About the Author

Susan Morem is a nationally recognized career and workplace expert. She is founder and president of Premier Presentation, Inc., a Minneapolis-based training and consulting firm. She has addressed audiences all over the United States on a wide variety of topics related to personal and professional development and has helped countless organizations bring a new level of professional behavior and awareness to their employees. Her client list includes many Fortune 500 companies, including Citibank, Coca-Cola, Honeywell, 3M, Sears, Target Stores, US Bank, and Wells Fargo.

Susan has appeared on a variety of television and radio programs and has been featured in numerous publications, including *The Wall Street Journal, USA Today, Chicago Sun-Times, The Dallas Morning News, and Glamour.* Her weekly workplace advice column appears in newspapers across the country and on the Internet.

Susan has created and been featured in nine internationally distributed training videos and is author of the book, *How to Gain the Professional Edge.*

When not working, she enjoys spending time with her husband, three daughters, and their dog.

For more information or to bring Susan into your company, conference, convention, or association gathering, call 763-557-4998 or e-mail her at sue@suemorem.com. You can also visit Susan's Web site at http://www.suemorem.com/.

Acknowledgements and Dedication

This book would not have been possible without the input of many people. Thank you, Petra Marquart, for your insight about the need for this book and suggesting I write it. Although I contemplated it for years, it was you who first put the idea in my head. Pamela Gould, thank you for your sincere interest and passion for what I do, and for connecting me with Ferguson Publishing Company.

Russ Beck, upon meeting you for the first time at Chicago's O'Hare Airport, I knew that Ferguson was the right publisher for this book. Russ, thank you for providing me with the opportunity and for everything you've done to make this book a success. I was completely reassured as we began creating the vision with Andrew Morkes. Andy, thank you for your keen insight and enthusiasm for this project. You gave me the freedom to take an idea and create it, and have beautifully captured my intent with your editing. Melissa Tucker, I can't thank you enough for hearing and really listening to my concerns and hopes for the outcome of this book, and your commitment to ensuring we met our objectives.

A big thanks to everyone who contributed to this book, including those of you who responded to surveys, shared your experiences and stories, and those who took the time to review the book before it was finished. A special thanks to Vault.com for providing me with up-to-the-minute information through its contacts and Web site.

To my friends, my daughters' friends, extended family members, and Blair Wilson, who is like a son, you have all remained interested in this project, listened to my ups and downs, and continue to be some of my biggest motivators. You have no idea how much your support really means to me.

To my parents, Rose and Jules Levin, my in-laws, Bev and Chuck Morem, my sister, Eileen Levin, and Jami Tish, who is like a sister, your pride and interest in my accomplishments and what I do mean more to me than you realize.

To my husband, soul mate, and best friend, Steve, without you and your never-ending support and encouragement, who knows what I would be doing! You are the best thing that ever happened to me.

And finally, to my three daughters, Stephanie, Stacie, and Samantha, the real inspiration behind this book and the second, third, and fourth best things that ever happened to me. This book is dedicated to you.

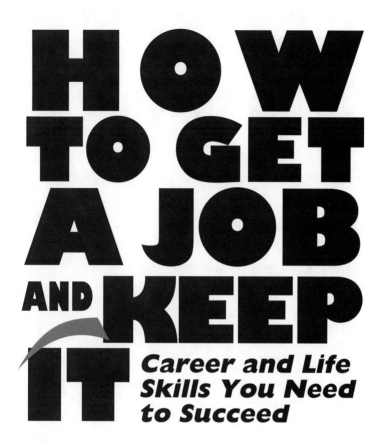

HOW TO GET A JOB AND KEEP IT

Career and Life Skills You Need to Succeed

SUSAN MOREM

FERGUSON PUBLISHING COMPANY
CHICAGO

Project Editor: Andrew Morkes
Proofreader: Barb Lightner
Indexer: Sandi Schroeder
Interior Design: The Glasoe Group
Cover Design: Sam Concialdi

Library of Congress Cataloging-in-Publication Data

Morem, Susan.
   How to get a job and keep it : career and life skills you need to
succeed / Sue Morem.
        p. cm.
Includes index.
   ISBN 0-89434-351-3 (pbk. : alk. paper)
  1. Job hunting. 2. Resumes (Employment) 3. Vocational guidance.
4. Career development. I. Title.
   HF5382.7 .M645 2001
   650.14--dc21

                                                    2001004022

Printed in the United States of America

Published and distributed by
Ferguson Publishing Company
200 West Jackson Boulevard, Suite 700
Chicago, Illinois 60606
800-306-9941
http://www.fergpubco.com

Table of Contents

Introduction

Stacie, my 15-year old daughter, was 20 minutes late for her new, summer job working with young children at a day camp. When her boss called our house to see where she was, I realized she had overslept and ran to her room to wake her. I assumed that my daughter would be grateful for my intervention. I was wrong. Stacie explained to me that she hadn't overslept but had planned on taking the day off.

When I asked her why she needed to take the day off after she had just made a commitment to work three days a week, Stacie thought she had a good reason. She told me that some of her friends were leaving to go out of town for a month, and she wanted to be at the airport to bid them farewell.

"Did your boss say it was okay?" I asked. "After all, aren't they counting on you to be there? Didn't you make a *commitment* to be there?" Stacie explained that she had left a voice message telling her boss that she wouldn't be there. "You told her, rather than *asked* her?" I inquired in growing disbelief.

I was stunned. My daughter had no idea that she had done something wrong and couldn't understand why I was so upset. I was upset and couldn't understand how she could be so irresponsible. She hadn't even thought about her responsibility to her boss and her new coworkers, although I suppose she thought she was being responsible by calling to say she wasn't coming to work that day.

A jumble of thoughts raced through my head. *What was she thinking? How could saying good-bye to friends at the airport be more important to her than going to work? Didn't she realize that people were depending on her? What kind of reference would she get for future jobs if she made a bad impression on this one? What about the commitment she made to this job?*

I finally got her to see the implications of her decision and convinced her to call and tell her boss that she would come in to work that day. When Stacie called, she discovered that her boss had never received the message she left because she had been too busy to check her voice mail.

This incident was a defining moment for me. Writing this book was something I sensed was needed, but now my hunch was confirmed. My *own* daughter had so little understanding as to what was expected of her in her job. There were and are so many things I realized I needed to tell her about the world of work. I began to think about all of the assumptions young and first-time employees make about their jobs and responsibilities. And all of the mistakes that could be avoided if someone just told them the basic rules of the workplace.

My daughter is a wonderful, intelligent person. She would never do anything to purposely upset anyone. She just didn't know. Yet how would she know? Who decides what she or anyone needs to know? Who would tell her? What class could she take? What book should she read? Until now, I wasn't sure. But I knew that there was something I could do to help.

I decided to talk with companies and learn about the challenges they are facing with young professionals. I also talked with young adults to learn about their concerns and determine how prepared they felt they were for the business world. My goals: discover what information was missing from the classroom and provide young people, via this book, with this necessary information before they enter the workplace for the first time.

As a young adult today you are savvy and, in many ways, far ahead of young adults from previous generations. You are also probably very independent and accustomed to fending for yourself due to the long working hours of your parents. From a young age, you were exposed to the Internet, voice mail, faxes, e-mail, buddy lists, television, PG-, PG-13- and R-rated movies. All of this exposure forces you to grow up very quickly. It is unfortunate because it may rob you of what could be an innocent childhood, and fortunate because these resources allow you to get a taste of the adult world before you become an adult yourself.

Whatever experiences or training you have had to this point, when you enter the business world, you most likely will discover that it is very different from the world you are used to. In school, if you miss a day of classes, you can find out what you missed and make up the work. The only person your absence affects is you. When you miss a day of work, you may not be able to make up what you missed, and your absence affects everyone you work with. The business world is fast paced and everyone's contribution—from entry-level clerk to company CEO—is important. People will be counting on you.

Being successful in a job is not necessarily the same as being successful in school. Employers look for more than just the completion of your work. There are many unspoken expectations in the workplace. Unspoken because employers assume you know what they want. There is far more to a job than just showing up for work. You need to literally show up in many ways. Employers want you to show up every day on time, looking good, enthused, positive, in a good mood, and ready to work. As basic as these expectations sound, it isn't easy for many people to show up in this manner. The people who do, however, have an advantage.

I don't think I've ever heard of anybody being criticized for being too positive or too professional, but I've heard a lot of criticism about people who are negative, moody, and difficult to get along with. You will have an advantage in the workplace and in life if you are pleasant and easy to deal with. People will like you and treat you well. Likability is essential in the business world and will increase your chances of promotion and success.

You are young and beginning a new phase of your life. You can be a breath of fresh air to your new coworkers on the job. Many of these people will be older and some may have lost their spark over the years. Some of them are stuck in a routine and experiencing stress in their lives. When a young and vibrant person such as yourself comes along, it can be very refreshing.

Looking for a job can be a full-time job in itself. You may tire of filling out applications, going on interviews, and wait-

> When you enter the business world, you most likely will discover that it is very different from the world you are used to.

ing for a response. You probably will breathe a sigh of relief when you are finally offered a job. You may even assume that once you are hired you can let your guard down, but beware, you are being observed every minute. Everything you do or don't do will impact your salary and your advancement opportunities.

> Everything you do or don't do will impact your salary and your advancement opportunities.

As you enter this new phase of your life, you may find yourself feeling pulled in many different directions. You may feel confident and knowledgeable. You may be eager to earn money and establish yourself as a financially independent adult. You may feel yourself changing and maturing, while some of your friends are not. There is a new side of you waiting to emerge, and I am confident that with a little preparation you will be where you need to be in no time. You will face obstacles and a few hurdles, but if you take a little time up front to prepare, you will enter the world of work equipped with the tools that will help you to succeed.

The transition from student to employee doesn't have to be difficult. I have written *How to Get a Job and Keep It: Career and Life Skills You Need to Succeed* to help you make this transition as easily as possible and to prepare you for what's ahead. So, what are we waiting for? Let's get started!

Section I:

Everything
You Need to Know
About Getting a Job

Chapter 1

How to Find and Land a Job

Test Your Job Search Skills

True, Sometimes True, or False?

1.

Who you know is more important than what you know.

2.

Employers look to hire people who have the highest grade point averages.

3.

An internship or volunteer work can help you overcome a lack of experience.

4.

When looking for a job, contact everyone you know as a way to increase your probability of generating additional contacts and job possibilities.

5.

Most people find a job within one month of beginning their job search.

6.

Try not to appear too eager for a position because you might appear as though you are desperate for work.

7.

Most jobs are found in newspaper advertisements.

8.

If you really want to work for a company, call and ask for an informational interview.

Test yourself as you read through this chapter. The answers appear on pages 32-35.

A New Beginning

My Story

I was so excited. I finally decided to leave school and look for a job. It had been a difficult decision to make. Part of me wanted to stay at the University of Minnesota. I loved campus life, but another part of me longed to get out in the real world and put some of the knowledge I had learned to use. I read every self-help book I could get my hands on and, after taking the Dale Carnegie course from Dale Carnegie Training, an internationally renowned corporate training company, I was confident I would make a better salesperson than student.

My parents always taught me that knowledge is power and have consistently been on a path of self-improvement. For years, my father sent many of the managers who worked for him through the Dale Carnegie course. In my second year of college, he offered to send me through the course. I, too, was always looking to grow and experience something new, so I jumped at the opportunity. My sister and I took the 14-week course together.

Although I was the youngest person in the class, I looked forward to attending each week. The class focused on communicating effectively, increasing confidence, influencing others, and coping with worry and stress. The course worked for me. I gained the confidence I needed to make this bold move.

I was determined to find a job in sales, a field I knew I would be good at. I loved people and had frequently heard comments reinforcing my natural sales ability. I worked part-time as a waitress, and spent the rest of my time looking for a job. I was excited about my future, but after a few weeks had gone by without a job offer, I became concerned. I had no idea that finding a job was a long process and soon learned that my search could last for months. I was extremely disillusioned.

I began my job search by reading the want ads in the newspaper. Most of the positions advertised required someone who either had experience or a college degree. I didn't have either, but that didn't stop me from responding to ads that sounded intriguing. My resume and cover letter must have triggered some interest because I was called in for a few interviews. Although I lacked some of the credentials these companies were looking for, I must have done something right in the interviews because I was asked back for second and third interviews.

Jim, a sales manager with a Fortune 500 company and one of the interviewers, told me that although I didn't have everything they were looking for in a candidate, I did have something special. "You know," he said, "I really think you would be great in this position. You've got great people skills, a good attitude, and lots of enthusiasm. Why don't you go get some sales experience under your belt and come back in a year?"

I was thrilled by his confidence in my ability, but a year seemed like an eternity. I couldn't understand why he wouldn't hire me and give me a chance to prove myself. I wanted to jump-start my career right then—not a year down the road. I heard the same thing over and over. Everyone thought I would be great in sales, and they all liked my confidence and my enthusiasm, but no one would give me a chance.

I began to dread Sundays. The newspaper would arrive with the new job listings in the employment section, and my search would begin all over again. All of the ads that sounded too good to be true *were* too good to be true. I could have found a job if I were willing to invest money or to work strictly on commission. But that wasn't what I wanted. I wanted a job with a regular paycheck. The jobs that didn't require experience did require a monetary investment, which I didn't have. I was losing momentum, my confidence, and, worst of all, I was losing what everyone said they liked best about me—my enthusiasm.

Experience Is the Best Teacher

How would I ever get work experience if no one would give me a chance? I was so frustrated! We all have to start somewhere, yet employers want to hire people with experience, so it becomes a vicious cycle. I kept asking myself, how do I get experience if I can't get a job?

Internships

I've since learned one way to gain experience, and it's by participating in an internship with a company while still in school. In fact, nearly 47 percent of executives who were polled rated professional experience as the most important quality in hiring new graduates. (The survey was developed by Office Team and conducted by an independent research firm.) Working as an intern or in a temporary position allows you to build your skills and business network and enhance your marketability to prospective employers. If you are able to acquire an internship, go for it, but if you can't, don't despair—you will find a job.

Build on Past Experiences

In trying to land my first real job, I realized I had to work with the experience I had. I began to evaluate everything I had done over the years. I had worked as a waitress for four years. Although this wasn't exactly sales experience or what employers wanted when they requested sales experience, I tried to sell my waitressing experience as a job that prepared me for a career in sales. After all, I learned a lot about people working as a waitress, and I gained experience working under pressure. In addition, I had one of the highest ticket averages, which I decided must be due to my sales ability.

I reviewed all of my past experiences. There was the neighborhood day camp I held in my backyard one summer and my brief experience as a consultant selling cosmetics. I was building on everything I had done and accomplished. I knew I could do the job, but I needed to convince the interviewers that I could.

I finally got the break I needed. I was doing some volunteering with the Dale Carnegie courses, and upon discovering that I was interested in a sales job, the people at Dale Carnegie offered me a position selling their training courses. What a perfect fit. The program that influenced me and changed the direction of my life was giving me an opportunity to prove myself and allow me to help other people change their lives in the process. I will always appreciate that opportunity. Just knowing that someone believed in me was so important. However, the job paid only straight commission, which meant I only made money when I sold something. Nevertheless, I realized that I could no longer be too selective. I needed to get experience and had to give something to gain something.

I worked for Dale Carnegie about a year, and after gaining the experience I needed, I went back to Jim at the Fortune 500

Seventy-six percent of the class of 2001 have completed at least one internship; 51 percent have completed two or more internships.

Source: Vault.com, Class of 2001 Survey

company that had been interested in me one year prior. I told him that I was still interested in working for him and that I now had the experience necessary to work for his company. I got the job and a chance to prove myself in the big leagues.

Follow Up and Follow Through

Jim could have easily forgotten me, but I wouldn't let him. Any job worth having is worth pursuing. You will be one of the lucky few if you have companies pursuing you. There are a few fields, such as computer science and engineering, that have difficulty finding qualified people. In some instances, there are more positions available than people to fill them, and some college students are being recruited long before they graduate.

While you are job hunting, you need to think of yourself as a salesperson. When you apply for a job, you are selling yourself.

Most of us, however, have to do our own searching and pursuing of a job. In any sales position, it is the salesperson's responsibility to follow up with a customer. While you are job hunting, you need to think of yourself as a salesperson. When you apply for a job, you are selling yourself. You need to follow up and follow through with everyone you deal with. You will be forgotten if you allow yourself to be.

Once you have an interview, you will want to follow up with the interviewer after it is over. If you want a job, you are going to have to show your interest. Don't expect to sit back and wait for the phone to ring. Go out and make things happen. You will feel a greater sense of control and get what you want much faster in the long run.

Venturing into Uncharted Territory

My experience in finding my first job was over 25 years ago. Looking through the want ads and calling people I knew were about the only ways to connect with others in order to find a job. Today, job seekers have a variety of search methods available to them. In fact, many available positions are never even advertised.

You, too, may find that your enthusiasm is waning at some point, and you may feel yourself becoming frustrated. Never give up. The job you want is out there. You just have to keep searching until you find it.

This is a new chapter in your life and a whole new experience you are embarking on. It is important that you know you will experience tough times. You will probably be rejected before you are accepted. Keep in mind that it isn't you, personally, that is being rejected. It may have more to do with job requirements, your level of training or experience, or the fact that someone else was a better fit for a particular position. If you don't get a job you really want, chances are there is a better opportunity yet to come.

Finding a Job Is a Job

The process involved in finding a job is like having a job. It is a process that is similar to starting your own business. You are in the business of finding a job. If you were to start your own business, you would need to set up an office and purchase some equipment. What would you need in that office? The following are some of the typical items necessary to run a business (or job search) effectively:

- Telephone
- Answering machine
- Fax machine
- Computer
- Printer
- Internet connection
- Stationary and envelopes
- Calendar/date book
- Pens, pencils

Some of these tools are essential, while others are optional. If you don't have a computer or fax machine, this isn't the time to purchase them if you can't afford to. As long as you have access to these things when you need them (via a library, friends, or at school), you will manage just fine.

Forty-eight percent of college seniors report that they have lost sleep because of their job search.

Source: Vault.com, Class of 2001 Survey

Establish a Routine

Plan on devoting a specific amount of time each day to the tasks of your job-hunting process. Try to establish a routine and stick to a schedule. Make a commitment to wake up at a certain time each day and determine a minimum amount of time you will commit to your job search. Make a certain number of calls every day to help you keep the momentum going. Develop a network of people you can count on to support you during this time and, if possible, meet with them on a regular basis.

Defining Your First Job

As you begin your quest to find your first job, I am willing to bet that this isn't your first job at all. How would you respond to the following questions?

- Have you ever earned an allowance? What did you do to earn it? Make your bed? Take out the garbage? Care for siblings or help around the house?
- Did you ever mow lawns or baby-sit for neighbors when you were young?
- Have you ever held a part- or full-time job?
- Did you ever work a summer job?

If you answered yes to any of these questions, then you've already had a job and have some experience working for someone else. However, most likely the kind of job you are about to look for now is quite a bit different from your previous jobs. After deciding on an industry and a career, you probably consider this to be your first *real* job search.

Plan on devoting a specific amount of time each day to the tasks of your job-hunting process.

Before you dismiss all of your previous work experience or assume that mowing lawns or baby-sitting doesn't count, I encourage you to evaluate what you've learned from your work experience thus far. First, list all of the jobs you have ever held. Then, ask yourself the following questions:

- What did I like best about my previous job(s)?
- What did I like least?
- What specific tasks did I perform?
- What was I really good at?
- What were some of the biggest challenges I faced, and how did I overcome them?
- What would I do differently today as a result of what I've learned?
- How did this experience impact me?

Spend some time answering these questions. (You might want to write down your responses to these questions on a sheet of paper in order to help you organize your thoughts.) When asked about a previous job in an interview, rather than saying, "I mowed lawns for my neighbors," think about all of the aspects of what you did and emphasize any unique aspects. For example, my neighbor Blair not only mowed lawns but found ways to add on to his mowing service by renting an aerator and aerating lawns in the spring. He was always looking for additional ways to grow his business. Tina, a childhood friend, not only baby-sat but did some basic filing for her employer's home business, too. Did you just baby-sit or mow lawns, or was there more to what you did?

It is important to identify the skills you've gained and transfer them to the job you are applying for.

Imagine an employer hearing a response like this: "I managed a yard service for four years. Each spring I made personal visits to over 40 houses in my neighborhood to solicit their yard business and determine their needs. As the business grew I hired others to assist me and gained experience in managing people. In addition, with so many homeowners working outside the home, I discovered that invoicing them was the best method of collecting payment. I created an invoicing program on my computer to facilitate billing. Overall, in addition to mowing lawns, I gained experience in running a small business." That's quite a different response than simply saying, "I mowed lawns for my neighbors."

It is important to identify the skills you've gained and transfer them to the job you are applying for. Look beyond the duties you performed and think about the accomplishments you made and what you learned as a result.

Perhaps you've had a challenging experience. You might talk about how you dealt with it and what you learned as a result. When my sister was 15, she accepted a job as a nanny for a family in our neighborhood. One day, the mother, who was going through a divorce and was depressed as a result, overdosed on her medication. She pushed a dresser against her door so that no one could get in. When she told my sister what she had done, my sister immediately called home, called an ambulance, and took the children out of the house.

If my sister were asked in an interview to relate a challenging experience and how she reacted to it, what might she say based on this incident? Think about it. She was dealing with life and death. She had to act fast, think on her feet, remain calm, and protect the young children.

What do you think my sister learned as a result? Perhaps she would say that we can never anticipate everything that might happen, but we need to be prepared for anything and be able to respond calmly and quickly. My sister showed that she was able to react quickly and think clearly under pressure. In addition, after the incident, my sister told the woman that she wouldn't baby-sit for her anymore if she ever did anything like that again—showing that she was able and willing to set boundaries.

Looking the Part

Taking a Risk

When I was 18, a friend of mine invited me to a cosmetics demonstration that she was hosting in her home. We sat around her dining room table, and Bonnie, an attractive young woman who was a beauty consultant, showed us how to properly cleanse our faces and apply make up. It was an enjoyable experience, and since I had never had any prior make up lessons, I learned lots of new tips.

At the end of the event, Bonnie recruited me to become a consultant and conduct the demonstrations myself. She thought I had all of the necessary ingredients to be successful as a beauty consultant, and I was both flattered and excited at this unique business opportunity.

I took out my first business loan and asked my family and friends to hold events for me. I also started using the skin care regime. To my horror, within a few weeks, I began to break out with a terrible case of acne. I called Bonnie and asked for advice. She didn't seem too surprised about my problem and told me that the product was working because it was removing the impurities in my skin.

As far as I was concerned, the impurities could stay in my skin. I looked awful and was worried about making claims that this product could improve the skin. Anyone who looked at me would see the contradiction. If the skin care regime worked so well, why didn't it work on my skin? I knew that there was no way I could stand before prospective buyers and make claims that they would have beautiful skin when, with one look at me, they would know I was lying. No one would want to go through what I did to have nice skin. I got out of the beauty consulting business as fast as I got in.

It was a painful experience, but I learned some very important lessons that have become the basis for what I currently do. I speak on professionalism, and one of the most important elements of a professional is to "look" the part of a professional.

I instinctively knew that I could not sell a skin care product and promise people beautiful skin with my skin in terrible condition. My message would be confusing since my skin didn't reflect what I was promising, and people wouldn't trust me.

That was the biggest lesson, but I learned much more about starting a business, recruiting people to become consultants, calling people to host parties, selling a product, and setting up an office. I kept thinking about my experiences and the lessons I learned until I was satisfied that I had skills that would help me sell myself to a prospective employer.

Internships and temporary assignments are ways to gain practical, on-the-job training while developing your professional skills.

Benefiting From Past Experience

If you wait to get experience and put off starting your career until after you get your degree, you may be at a disadvantage. In a survey developed by Office Team, 47 percent of executives polled rated professional experience as the most important quality in hiring new graduates, even more than the type of degree earned (18 percent) or grade point average (17 percent). Another survey, developed by Accountemps, reported that 93 percent of the chief financial officers interviewed said it is important for entry-level accountants to have gained experience in the field prior to graduation.

As mentioned earlier, internships and temporary assignments are ways to gain practical, on-the-job training while developing your professional skills. Everything you have done or accomplished up to this point will help you as you begin to define yourself for prospective employers. Think about your answers to the following questions:

- What volunteer work have I done?
- Am I or have I been involved in any school or outside organizations?
- What leadership positions have I held?
- What awards or special recognition have I received?

An experience doesn't have to pay you money for it to have value and impact. Spend some time thinking about all of your accomplishments and what you've gained and learned as a result.

Making Important Decisions

Choosing a career is one of the most important decisions you will make and is not something to be decided on a whim. By the time you begin looking for a job you hopefully will have done some career planning and taken steps to ensure your education has prepared you for your chosen career. The process you are about to begin is not to be taken lightly. You want to be sure you make the right choice when you accept a job.

Many people tend to move around quite a bit with part-time jobs that they held during high school or college, yet some people stick with the same company or job for years. The stability that comes from working at a job long term can be attractive to a prospective employer, but if you have changed jobs frequently it isn't necessarily a detriment.

Although most people can expect to change jobs a number of times in the span of their careers, each job they hold can last for years.

An experience doesn't have to pay you money for it to have value and impact.

If you choose a full-time position that offers advancement and growth opportunities, you will only be able to grow within that organization if you stick around awhile. While job hopping when you are a student isn't always viewed negatively, once you are a full-time employee, it may present a few challenges.

It isn't necessarily negative to move around a bit, but when it is excessive you may find it difficult to explain to potential employers, and it could raise a red flag. Even though employers aren't always loyal to their workers, they want to believe their employees will be loyal to them.

Cam Marston of Marston Communications, a mother-and-son consulting team, says that he has heard complaints that young professionals are no longer loyal to their workplace. Although some people would view this as a negative, Marston says it is actually a good characteristic. "Young professionals have learned that they are solely responsible for their success. Blind loyalty to the company will not get them where they want to go. It is important to understand that in the new workplace, career advancement is a responsibility of the individual, not the HR department or their boss," Marston says.

Take charge of your career. Accepting a job isn't a lifelong commitment, but the decision shouldn't be made too lightly. You may be tempted to accept the first offer that comes along or the job that offers you the most money, but you will be much happier if you wait for the job that has what you are looking for.

Accepting a job isn't a lifelong commitment, but the decision shouldn't be made too lightly.

There are unique circumstances surrounding the search for a first job. You may or may not know exactly what you need or want from a job. Other than receiving a paycheck and utilizing your knowledge and skills in your chosen field, you may become confused as you view all of your job options.

Evolution of a Professional

Find a Mentor

Long before you begin your job search, you need to begin to evolve into a professional person. It is important to evaluate who you are and who you need to become to fit the role you are taking on and to fit into the business environment you want to work in. Rather than trying to make this transition all by yourself, it will be much easier if you find someone to help you.

A frequent comment I've heard from the executives I interviewed for this book was that young people need a mentor—someone who is willing to take you under their wings and not only provide advice but spend time helping you grow. A mentor may be a family member or friend or even someone you currently don't know. He or she could be someone in the industry you are interested in or a friend of a friend. Many companies have implemented mentoring programs, but until you have a job, you are on your own to find a mentor.

As you begin talking with people about your chosen profession, you will acquire valuable information as well as additional contacts. Each contact will lead to another contact, so don't be hesitant to ask for names and phone numbers. It's always easier calling someone when you have a friend in common than calling someone when you don't have anything or anyone in common. Learning more about the career you are interested in is all about networking with others. It's probably how you've met many of your friends. Someone introduced you to someone else; that's what networking is all about.

Use Your Network of People

My oldest daughter, Stephanie, was nearing the end of her high school years and becoming serious about her search for the right college. But it wasn't until she began talking with others that she got some of her most valuable information. She would hear about a school and express interest in learning more about it and, sure enough, someone knew someone who went there. Happily, they would provide her with the name, telephone number, and e-mail address of that person. She was able to get all of her questions answered about that school once she connected with someone who went there.

You may have heard the adage "It's not who you know, it's what you know." In other words, talking with and knowing the right people is important. Don't let the word "networking" worry you. Networking is just a fancy word for talking with people, forming relationships, asking the right questions, and getting the information you need. You talk to people every day. You may already be networking with some people or you may be overlooking the possibilities that can evolve merely from asking the right questions of casual and not-so-casual acquaintances.

To successfully network, you must be willing to talk with people outside of your circle of acquaintances.

To successfully network, you must be willing to talk with people outside of your circle of acquaintances. This is the only way to effectively network and connect with the right people. For example, assume you are interested in advertising. You don't really know anyone in the field but recall that a friend's brother works in advertising. Will you be willing to call this friend and ask for his or her brother's telephone number? In addition to friends, you can network with teachers, members of your church, synagogue, or mosque, neighbors, relatives, and people who belong to a variety of organizations.

You Are a Gift

You are young, and this is an exciting time of your life. You are most likely enthusiastic, idealistic, and excited about the end-less possibilities you have before you. There are aspects of your youth that will benefit you as you enter the business world. There are other aspects that could potentially interfere with your job opportunities and undermine your best intentions.

Please don't worry about losing yourself in the process. Think of yourself as a gift to any company lucky enough to employ you. You may simply need some repackaging. There are many gifts for employers to choose from. How can you best convince a prospec-tive employer that you are the best gift for the company?

If you had two wrapped gifts placed in front of you and you were only able to open one of them, how would you decide which one to unwrap? Very likely, the packaging would influence you. If one of the gifts were beautifully and profes-sionally wrapped, and the other were haphazardly wrapped with wrinkled, recycled paper, which one would you choose as the gift you wanted to open and why?

Selling Yourself

Whether you consider yourself a salesperson or not, when you are looking for a job you are trying to sell yourself to a prospec-tive employer. There are several areas that are part of your package and "seen" by prospective employers.

What words do you use when describing yourself? Do you speak favorably of yourself and your accomplishments? Every word you use when you talk about yourself paints a picture of who you are in the mind of others. To effectively sell yourself, you must know yourself. Take some time to think about and respond to the following questions. (Write your answers on a separate sheet of paper.)

- What three words best describe the way you see yourself?
- What three words describe you as you would like to see yourself?
- If the words differ, what do you need to do so that the two sets of descriptions match—so that you are who you want to be?
- What are three of your best qualities?
- What are three areas you need to improve upon?
- What accomplishment are you most proud of?
- How would your friends describe you?
- How would your family describe you?
- How would a previous employer describe you?
- How would one of your teachers describe you?
- Why should someone hire you?

Spend time thinking about and practicing your responses to these questions. Be prepared to talk about yourself positively and enthusiastically. This will be essential as you meet people, network, and interview. In addition, know what skills you possess and be willing to talk about them. Don't assume others know your strengths or skills and don't underestimate or take your skills for granted. Peter Vogt, a career counselor and the Campus Career Coach for Monster.com, says that many new graduates take their computer skills for granted and don't realize, for example, that the ability to do research on the Internet is a marketable skill. They think that "everyone can do that" because their only points of reference are their fellow students. Vogt says that many people in the business world don't possess this skill. So it's critical, as a student, to play up your computer skills and to continuously learn new ones. Even if you don't feel you're going into a computer-related field, you'll stand out in any workplace if you have good computer skills.

Be prepared to talk about yourself positively and enthusiastically. This will be essential as you meet people, network, and interview.

Use the Right Words

One common piece of advice among many experts on successful resume writing and interviewing is to use the right words when describing yourself and your accomplishments.

Find and use the right words to describe your qualities and accomplishments.

As you read the following words, circle those that describe you best.

Note: If you do not own this copy of *How to Get a Job and Keep It*, then be sure to make a photocopy of this page and mark up the copy.

Accurate	Extroverted	Organized
Achiever	Flexible	Original
Aggressive	Forceful	Outgoing
Approachable	Friendly	Outspoken
Arrogant	Gentle	Polite
Assertive	Gracious	Positive
Committed	Humble	Precise
Competitive	Impatient	Receptive
Confident	Independent	Reserved
Considerate	Influential	Respectful
Controlling	Intellectual	Restless
Creative	Intelligent	Restrained
Daring	Introverted	Sarcastic
Dedicated	Intuitive	Self-centered
Dependable	Leader	Self-reliant
Determined	Loyal	Soft-spoken
Diplomatic	Motivational	Supportive
Disciplined	Naïve	Tactful
Dynamic	Negative	Team player
Energetic	Obedient	Tolerant
Enthusiastic	Open-minded	Trustworthy
Entrepreneurial	Optimistic	Versatile

Look at the words you circled and cross off any that you believe are unflattering characteristics—words that you would want to avoid using in an interview or in the workplace when describing yourself.

Next, read through the same list again, and this time circle only the words that you think are valuable traits of successful people in the workplace.

Accurate	Extroverted	Organized
Achiever	Flexible	Original
Aggressive	Forceful	Outgoing
Approachable	Friendly	Outspoken
Arrogant	Gentle	Polite
Assertive	Gracious	Positive
Committed	Humble	Precise
Competitive	Impatient	Receptive
Confident	Independent	Reserved
Considerate	Influential	Respectful
Controlling	Intellectual	Restless
Creative	Intelligent	Restrained
Daring	Introverted	Sarcastic
Dedicated	Intuitive	Self-centered
Dependable	Leader	Self-reliant
Determined	Loyal	Soft-spoken
Diplomatic	Motivational	Supportive
Disciplined	Naïve	Tactful
Dynamic	Negative	Team player
Energetic	Obedient	Tolerant
Enthusiastic	Open-minded	Trustworthy
Entrepreneurial	Optimistic	Versatile

Now compare the two lists. What traits did you circle in the second list (your perception of successful people) that you didn't circle in the first list (your perception of yourself)? What can you do to develop these successful traits?

It is important to see yourself as you want to be and to incorporate words representing the traits you desire into your vocabulary. You will be selling your skills and qualities. Choose your descriptive words carefully so that you convey the right message.

Inside the Package

A resume is the first part of the package an employer sees; therefore, it is essential that your resume represents you well. An employer sees a glimpse of who you are through your resume and can see your background, including your education, work history, and interests. Your resume should represent you well. If it doesn't, you may never get the opportunity for an interview. Even if you pass this test, you won't be getting a job offer from just your resume. The objective is for your resume to sell you well enough to be granted an interview.

Suggestion: Your resume is the first impression a prospective employer has of you. Make sure it represents you professionally and accurately. (More on resumes in Chapter 2.)

Your Image

Once you are granted an interview, you can assume that your credentials were sufficient to get to this step. Now, the employer wants to meet you to see if your image reflects your resume and fits the picture of the person he or she is looking for. Your image is conveyed through your clothing, body language, and facial expressions. How will you package yourself?

Suggestion: Pay close attention to your clothing, body language, and facial expressions to ensure you present the best image.

Your Communication Skills

Assuming your image is on par, are you an effective communicator? How you sound in person, on the phone, in e-mail, and on your answering machine is a part of your professional package.

If someone calls to set up an interview, and your answering machine plays a rap song or conveys off-color humor, what message will that send to a prospective employer?

If you plan on giving out your e-mail address and communicating on the Internet, you'll want to evaluate your e-mail address. Asking a potential employer to contact you at Partygirl.com or Egomaniac.net may send the wrong message, especially during this critical time of initial assessment.

An employer sees a glimpse of who you are through your resume and can see your background, including your education, work history, and interests.

Suggestion: Take a look at the many ways you communicate and see to it that all of your communication tools represent you as a professional—not the teen or student you have been but the person you are becoming.

Taking a Risk

You and your employer will be taking a risk if you decide to work together. With little to go on, an employer can only hope that you will fit into his or her particular work environment and, hopefully, meet and exceed expectations.

Think very carefully about the kind of job you want. Although you may be motivated by salary, money isn't and shouldn't be the only reason you accept a job. When you begin working full-time, you will be spending, on average, 40 hours a week at this job. You will be spending more time working than doing anything else, except maybe sleeping. You may as well spend your time doing something you enjoy.

Although you may be motivated by salary, money isn't and shouldn't be the only reason you accept a job.

People who work full-time crave balance in their lives. You undoubtedly have developed interests and hobbies over the years. You shouldn't have to give up everything you love doing because you work full-time. You will want to find a job that enables you to have balance in your life and to pursue those things that are most important to you.

I know of many people who earn large amounts of money who are not necessarily the happiest people. Money is not the only way to have a happy life. Happiness is a choice that comes as a result of making the right decisions. If you happen to earn a good living doing the things that make you happy, so much the better.

Deciding What You Want to Do

I was invited to speak to a group of 20 high school seniors who were part of an experimental business preparation class. I was asked to speak about Etiquette. Before I began, everyone had a chance to introduce him- or herself, and tell me what they were going to do with their futures. "I'm going into interior design," one young woman responded. "Entertainment," the next person said. It went on: sports management, law, marketing, theater . . . every person in attendance knew what they wanted to pursue. I was amazed and impressed that these 17- and 18-year-olds knew exactly what they wanted to do in their professional lives. When I was a senior in high school, if you asked me what I wanted to do with my life, my answer would have been, "Graduate!"

You may or may not yet know what you want to do with your life, but at some point you will have to make that decision. Many young people envision themselves working for a large company. According to the book, *The Very Quick Job Search* (JIST Works, 1995), 71 percent of employees work for small companies (companies employing 1-249 people), 16 percent work for medium-sized companies (250-999 people), and only 13 percent work for large companies (1,000 employees or more).

Maybe you know what you want to do with the rest of your life, but if you don't, don't despair. Perhaps you are the type who likes to see where life takes you. Or maybe you have an idea but aren't really sure.

Whatever stage of discovery you are in, you've got plenty of time and more resources than ever before available to find and discover what is out there for you. Use these resources to your advantage.

Using the Internet

One of the fastest growing and most easily accessible job search tools is the Internet. The Internet has even impacted the job-interview process, according to John Kador, who wrote an article on interviewing for *InfoWorld,* a computer industry trade magazine. He says that hiring managers have had to develop new questions to screen applicants for information technology skills and business savvy. It is important to be comfortable with technology, and using it in your job search can be to your advantage.

There are thousands of Web sites related to career exploration. There are sites designed to

- Help you assess and identify your goals, skills, and interests.
- Learn about specific occupations.
- Determine where to acquire the necessary education and training for an occupation.

Maybe you know what you want to do with the rest of your life, but if you don't, don't despair.

- Determine if licenses or certifications are necessary for certain occupations.
- Create and design a resume and cover letter.
- Put together a career portfolio.
- Find job openings.
- Negotiate a job offer.

A listing of some of the more useful career Web sites can be found on page 29.

Informational Interviews

If you are lucky enough to be connected with someone who works in your desired field, call and ask for an informational interview. This is quite different from an interview for a position. The purpose of this type of meeting is to gain information and expand your network.

Come to an informational interview prepared.

An informational interview gives you an opportunity to meet people and learn about companies you may want to work for. What better way to learn about a career than to talk to people who are actually doing that career already?

If you don't have any contacts in the industry you are interested in working in but are interested in obtaining an informational interview, call the human resources department of a company in that field. There is always a chance that you may be turned down, but you might be surprised at how helpful many people are willing to be.

Come to an informational interview prepared. Prepare a list of questions to ask. This type of interview enables you to find out about a typical day on the job, what the person enjoys or dislikes, and much more. Some questions you might ask are:

- How did you get into this line of work?
- What experience and requirements are needed to work in this field?
- When hiring, what do you look for in job candidates?
- What's the best way to break into this field or industry?
- What is a typical day like?
- What sets your company apart from the competition?
- What can you tell me about the corporate culture?
- How do you typically post job openings or find people to work here?

Useful Web Sites

Career and Industry Research

America's CareerInfoNet (http://www.acinet.org/acinet/)

U.S. Bureau of Labor Statistics (http://stats.bls.gov/)

Salary

*National Occupational Employment and Wage
   Estimates* (http://stats.bls.gov/oesnl/oes_alph.htm)

Salary.com (http://www.salary.com/)

Wageweb (http://www.wageweb.com/)

Networking/Information Interviewing

Monster.com (http://content.monster.com/network/)

Internships

InternshipPrograms.com

(http://internships.wetfeet.com/home.asp)

Career Planning

Jobweb (http://www.jobweb.com/)

Monster.com (http://www.monster.com)

Vault.com (http://www.vault.com/)

Job Listings

America's JobBank (http://www.ajb.org/)

BestJobsUSA (http://www.bestjobsusa.com/index-jsk-ie.asp)

CareerExposure (http://www.careerexposure.com/)

MonsterTRAK.com (http://www.jobtrak.com)

Cover Letters

CareerLab

(http://www.careerlab.com/letters/default_new2_left.htm)

Quintessential Careers.

(http://www.quintcareers.com/cover_letter_tutorial_map.html)

Interviewing

Job-interview.net (http://www.job-interview.net/)

Companies

Hoovers (http://www.hoovers.com/)

WetFeet.com (http://www.wetfeet.com/asp/home.asp)

Don't forget that everyone you interview is very busy and will be taking precious time away from their work to answer your questions. Respect the time of your interviewee by keeping your informational interview to one hour or less.

You will want to look and act professional in order to make a positive impression. In addition, don't hesitate to ask for feedback on your qualifications for this field and for a referral to someone who might be of further assistance.

Always send a note thanking the person for his or her time. Conducting informational interviews can be useful while still in school or when you are looking for a job.

Other Resources

Talking with people is one of the best ways to learn more about what interests you and what resources are available. If you haven't already, use the career/counseling/placement office at your school. It may offer a variety of tests to assess everything from your interests to your personality profile.

Employment agencies can be a good resource as well. There are several different types of agencies. Some charge a fee for their services and job placement, and others charge the employer the fee once you've found a job. Most will work with you in your development as well, helping you assess your skills, personality, and ability.

Patience Is a Virtue

As I conducted my research to determine some of the biggest challenges companies face with young, first-time professionals, patience was a common theme. "These kids come out of school expecting a lot," says Richard Lerner, CEO of RLM Public Relations in New York City, "and they don't always realize how much is ahead of them. They are motivated to get raises and expect to get them—fast."

You have grown up in one of the strongest periods of economic growth in recent history. You are used to things happening fast, but in the business world, patience is a virtue. As you search for a job, be patient and wait for the right job before you accept a position. Stay motivated and don't become

As you search for a job, be patient and wait for the right job before you accept a position. Stay motivated and don't become discouraged if your job search takes longer than expected.

discouraged if your job search takes longer than expected. Although weeks can seem like months, the time you spend looking for a job is relatively brief compared to the number of years you will be working.

Again, think of looking for a job as a job. Take your job search seriously and set yourself up to succeed. You will continue to evolve, improve, and learn. Every person you talk with is another person you can learn from. Every company you learn about expands your understanding of the business world. The attitude you adopt now will carry over into your career. You will have ups and downs in both your job search and your career. There will be good days and bad days, stressful days and easy days. Try to be realistic in what lies ahead for you. You may not find exactly what you want in your first job. Be patient; enjoy the process and the journey that lies ahead.

Test Your Job Search Skills

Questions and Answers

True, Sometimes True, or False?

1.

Who you know is more important than what you know.

Sometimes true. It's a good idea to work with anyone you know who may be able to help you find a job. It's always nice to have an introduction into a company and especially nice to have a personal recommendation or referral. But don't worry if you are lacking the connections to make this happen. Many people find their own jobs, and you can, too. However, if you have people "in the know," don't be too proud to ask for help.

2.

Employers look to hire people who have the highest grade point averages.

False. In very specialized industries, your grade point average may determine whether you are hired or not, but in most hiring situations, a high grade point average will not guarantee you a job offer. You may be terrific at taking tests, but how does that demonstrate your ability to communicate effectively or work well with others? When you are interviewing for a job, you need to offer more than your school smarts. You need to be business smart as well.

3.

An internship or volunteer work can help you overcome a lack of experience.

True. College students who decide to wait until they've earned their degrees to begin their careers may be at a professional disadvantage. In a recent Office Team survey, 47 percent of executives polled rated professional experience as the most important quality in hiring new graduates.

An internship is no longer a "choice" or an "elective" for college students. It has basically become a requirement, according to Peter Vogt, who has this to say: "From an employer's perspective, a college student or new graduate who relies solely on his or her education is someone to be passed over for another student/graduate who has supplemented his/her education with practical, real-world experience(s). Companies and organizations have too much to do and too little time and money to invest in teaching you what you should have learned, in their opinion, in college."

4.

When looking for a job, contact everyone you know as a way to increase your probability of generating additional contacts and job possibilities.

True. The more people you have helping you, the better. The more people who know you are looking for work, the better your chances of hearing about opportunities. It is estimated that as much as 70 percent of all positions will be found as a direct result of contacting other people. It's called *networking*—making your network of people work for you. Obviously, there are effective and ineffective methods of networking. Simply calling people to inform them you are in the job market is not effective networking. Contacting people in a particular field or with a specific request will be much more effective. You may be surprised to learn that people will be happy to refer you to someone that can be of additional help and that most people are happy to help. Get the word out and increase your chances of connecting with the right people.

5.

Most people find a job within one month of beginning their job search.

False. You will be very lucky if you are able to find a job that you want and receive an offer within one month of beginning your job search. Typically, the process takes much longer. Two to three months is average, but it can take up to six months or even longer.

Don't feel rushed to make a decision if you are offered a job that doesn't seem to match your abilities or needs. Take the time to make the right decision.

6.

Try not to appear too eager for a position because you might appear as though you are desperate for work.

Sometimes true. You want to show your enthusiasm and interest in a position, but don't want to appear desperate for a couple of reasons. You could lose your negotiating power or seem pushy. There should be a balance in the interview process. The company should be interested in you and you should be interested in it.

For example, if a company really wants to hire you and pursues you aggressively, but you are not interested, the pursuit could annoy you.

Don't be afraid to express your interest, but take each step slowly and calmly.

7.

Most jobs are found from newspaper advertisements.

False. Research has found that many job openings are never advertised. According to *USA Today,* only 14 percent of all jobs are found from advertisements. In fact, many job openings are never even advertised. As many as 70 percent of all professional jobs are filled through personal contacts and networking.

This doesn't mean that you shouldn't read the want ads, but if you want to increase your chances of finding a job, you will need to do more than scan newspaper ads. There are many available resources: the Internet, career placement offices, employment agencies, contacting companies directly, and using your own network of people.

8.

If you really want to work for a company, call and ask for an informational interview.

True. Even if you are told that there are no positions available, ask for an informational interview. Many people will be willing to take the time to talk with you, and an informational interview will give you an opportunity to learn about different companies and develop contacts. If you make a good impression, a lead or future opportunity may be the result. Come prepared with a few questions, keep the appointment brief (15 to 20 minutes), and be gracious for the opportunity.

Chapter Summary

To Maximize Your Job Search:

✓ **Treat finding a job as a job.** Set up a special workstation for your job search, and follow a schedule to ensure you spend some time each day pursuing new contacts and advancing your job possibilities.

✓ **Discover what you've gained from your work experience.** Evaluate every job you've held and identify what you learned as a result. Be prepared to talk about this in interviews.

✓ **Put on your selling shoes.** You are the product, and need to sell yourself to potential employers. No one can sell you as well as you can sell yourself. Be your own advocate.

✓ **Identify the words that define who you are.** Recognize your strengths and your weaknesses. Be prepared to talk about yourself. Know who you are and who you want to be.

✓ **Follow up and follow through.** Follow up with everyone you speak with, and always thank anyone who has helped you in any way. If you say you will get back to someone, make sure you do. Nothing discredits you more than not doing something that you say you will do.

✓ **Maximize your network.** Connect with as many people as possible. Ask everyone you know for contacts to help expand your network.

✓ **Use all your available resources.** Utilize the services that are provided: school or college career centers, friends, family, guidance counselors, teachers, internship possibilities, and the Internet.

✓ **Be patient.** Don't expect things to happen overnight. You will find a job, but it may take some time. Remember that all good things are worth waiting for.

Chapter 2

Putting Yourself on Paper

True, False, or Depends?

1.

In order to make your resume stand out from others, print it on brightly colored paper.

2.

A resume never should exceed one page.

3.

It is not necessary to submit a cover letter with your resume.

4.

It is fine to lie a little on your resume if it will help you get an interview.

5.

It is best to submit your resume by e-mail.

6.

A resume should not be folded.

7.

If you don't have access to a computer, you can hand write your resume as long as your handwriting is neat and legible.

8.

To help personalize your resume, include a picture of yourself.

9.

The more references you have, the better, so include as many as you can on your resume.

10.

Don't call a potential employer after submitting a resume. You will be called if you are qualified for the position.

Test yourself as you read through this chapter. The answers appear on pages 50-53.

Creating a Resume

A resume is the first thing an employer sees and is part of the first impression someone will have of you. A poorly written or produced resume will end up in a file or pile somewhere, or worse yet, in the trash. It is essential to have your resume represent you in the best possible manner.

It is essential to have your resume represent you in the best possible manner.

As we've already discussed, you need to think of yourself as a gift to an employer and do your best to package yourself effectively. When you receive a gift, a card usually comes with it. Some people walk into a store and buy the first card they see. Others take their time and look through a number of cards, selecting only the perfect card for the occasion.

Your resume is like the card you send with a gift. If you send the most appropriate one you should get the results and reaction you want. A resume is not something that should be completed too quickly or without outside help. A resume should include your:

- Objective (the position you are applying for, what your talents are, and so on)
- Qualifications
- Education
- Skills
- Academic accomplishments
- Personal accomplishments
- Work experience (responsibilities, accomplishments)
- Employment history
- Contact information (telephone numbers, street and e-mail addresses)

Your resume represents the best of who you are, and if prepared properly, it will be successful in securing interviews for you.

In addition, think of your resume as a business or calling card. It is important to include your name, address, telephone number, and e-mail address so that, if interested, someone will know how to get in touch with you. Make it easy for prospective employers to connect with you (especially during business hours), by providing them with as much information as possible.

Resume Web Sites and Books

Web Sites

College Grad Job Hunter
  (http://www.collegegrad.com/resumes/)
Rebecca Smith's eResumes and Resources
  (http://www.eresumes.com/)
10 Minute Resume
  (http://www.10minuteresume.com)

Books

Gallery of Best Resumes. Second Edition. (David F. Noble, JIST Works, 2000)
Resumes for Dummies. (Joyce Lain Kennedy, Hungry Minds, 2000)
Resumes That Knock'Em Dead. (Martin John Yate, Adams Media, 2000)

It is wise to work with someone as you prepare your resume. Utilize as many of the services and information available to you as possible. There are wonderful books written about resume writing, a number of Internet sites with valuable information, and resumes services that will, for a fee, help you put together your resume. Take time to do some research before you begin to create your resume.

What Are You Looking For?

Imagine that you are looking to hire someone to help you with your job search. You want to make your decision carefully because this person will be instrumental in helping you identity what you want to do, assist you in developing your resume, help you connect with companies, and much more. You place an ad and receive a number of letters and resumes as a result. In fact the response to your ad is so great that you have to find an efficient way to determine which responses are worth pursuing.

As you glance through the pile of resumes, you notice that most are on plain white or off-white paper, but a few are on different shades—one is bright orange. Most are written in 10- to 14-point type and use standard fonts such as Helvetica, Times Roman, and Palatino. One resume features a variety of font sizes and styles that really makes it stand out.

The majority of the resumes are just one page, a few are two pages, and one is about three pages long. A few are folded, some are stapled, and one is taped together. In addition to the resume, several applicants have included a letter, personally written to you, stating their interest in helping you find a job. You notice a misspelled word here and there and an incomplete sentence on one resume. One person has included a picture of himself with his resume, and another has listed personal data such as age, height, and weight.

The response has been so great that you realize you won't have time to meet with more than three or four people. You want to get this person working for you sooner rather than later. You can't put off your search any longer.

You never have a second chance to make a first impression.

How will you determine which people you want to take the time to meet with? What criteria will you use? Remember, the only information you have at this point is a resume from each person.

As you review the resumes, do you think you will:
- Disregard one if there is a coffee stain on it?
- Read every word on every resume to determine who is most qualified?
- Skim and scan the resumes to determine which ones you want to pursue?
- Trash the ones that lack creativity and read only those resumes that were composed using an unusual font or printed on colored paper?
- Read those with cover letters first?
- Pursue the one who sent the picture?
- Laugh off those with typographical errors?

Take time to think about your answers because it will help you as you make decisions about the resume you create. When you submit your resume to companies, it will be one of hundreds that employers will see. You want to be certain that your resume will sell you effectively and help you to be selected for an interview.

Most Common Mistakes

Susan Britton Whitcomb, author of *Resume Magic: Trade Secrets of a Professional Resume Writer* (JIST Works, 1998), defines a resume as an advertisement that should appeal to an employer's specific needs. According to Whitcomb, some of employers' biggest pet peeves and the most common mistakes made on resumes include:

- Leaving out dates
- No chronological listing of work experience
- No listing of accomplishments
- Incomplete listing of accomplishments
- Fancy fonts
- Photos
- Typos
- Misspelled words
- Disorganized structure
- Too long

Proofread, Proofread, Then Proofread Again

Have you ever written a paper, looked it over, and submitted it, confident it was error free, and discovered afterward that it had a typo or mistake you overlooked?

Any document that you work on for a long time eventually becomes difficult to view objectively. Since your resume is your future, it is even more difficult to be objective. It is a good idea to have several people (trusted friends, your parents, or a teacher) proofread your resume before submitting it to ensure it is error free. The more people you have look it over, the better your chances that you will catch any and all mistakes.

I write a nationally syndicated workplace advice column and am always under a deadline to get it in on time for publication. If I wait too long to write it, I don't have the time necessary to view it with a critical eye. On occasion I have turned in a column assuming it was fine, only to discover after it had been sent that there were several mistakes. Although many of

You want to be certain that your resume will sell you effectively and help you to be selected for an interview.

the mistakes were minor, and it is easy to see how they were overlooked, occasionally I will notice a mistake that is so obvious that it is hard to believe I didn't catch it myself.

When we don't take time to step away from a document, we lose our ability to be objective. Always allow yourself time to step away from any document you are working on before you conduct your final edit. It is even better if you do this on several different occasions. Each time you come back to it you are likely to see something you didn't see before.

Resumania is the term hiring expert Robert Half, founder of Accountemps, a staffing service, coined to describe the blunders that appear in resumes, job applications, and cover letters. Hiring managers who receive documents with mistakes, misused words, or inappropriate information may toss them, or worse yet, put them in their own Resumania file. The following are a few examples of real resume blunders:

- Worked party-time as an office assistant
- Planned and held up meetings
- Thank you for beeting me for an interview
- Computer illiterate
- I am entirely through in my work; no detail gets by me

Always allow yourself time to step away from any document you are working on before you conduct your final edit.

You want your resume to generate interest, not laughs. Take the time to make sure your resume is error free.

E-Mail or Snail-Mail?

It is easy to assume that with the capabilities of the Internet the preferred way to send a resume would be e-mail. In a recent survey of executives, nearly 50 percent of the respondents said their firm's preference was to receive resumes via e-mail. This is a substantial turnaround from just two years ago, when only 4 percent said they favored this method.

The survey was conducted by an independent research firm and was developed by Office Team, a leading staffing service. The executives were also asked what percent of resumes they receive via e-mail, and the mean response was 34 percent.

"The Internet enables you to get your credentials directly into the hands of hiring managers and may give you an advantage over less immediate delivery methods," says Diane Domeyer, executive director of Office Team. When sending a resume electronically, she recommends sending it both as an attachment and as text and to include the position of interest and your name in the subject line. Make sure you label your resume attachment with your name as well. Receiving hundreds of documents titled "resume" can be confusing to a prospective employer.

You may want to ask your potential employer the preferred way of sending a resume if you have the opportunity, but if an e-mail address is listed and sending it electronically is requested, you needn't worry. However, it doesn't hurt to send it by regular mail as well, or better yet, to hand deliver it if at all possible.

The Perfect Presentation

Hand delivering a resume assures you that it will arrive in perfect condition. Remember, this is your one chance to make a great impression. You don't want to submit a damaged resume, and want to make sure it looks good when it gets into the hands of the right person.

To Fold or Not to Fold

Can you imagine receiving a folded birthday or holiday card? It is highly unlikely. There are numerous sizes of greeting cards and just as many sizes of envelopes. Folding a resume is not recommended, nor is stapling or taping sheets together. Purchase envelopes that are the same size as the paper you are using.

Colors, Paper, and Keeping It Clean

Neutral colors (white, off-white, pale gray) are most commonly used for resumes and are preferred by employers. Print your resume on high quality paper and make sure there are no marks or stains on your resume.

Easy to Read

Your resume should be easy to read and easy to scan. It is estimated that employers will glance at your resume and decide within seconds whether it is worth reading, so your resume

must be visually appealing and easy to read. Bulleted information is one way to make a resume easy to read. So is using a
larger point size (but not too large) and keeping your resume
to one page, if possible.

Do what you can to make your resume distinctive, but
don't make it too unusual or you may not be taken seriously.
Some people will do anything to make their resume stand out,
but less can be more. Think understated and professional,
rather than overstated and wildly creative.

The Truth and Nothing But the Truth

You may be tempted to tell a little lie in order to make yourself
sound and look better, but resist the temptation. Imagine
working at a job that, in essence, you got dishonestly. After
working awhile, the lie is uncovered. If that were to happen
not only would you lose the trust of your employer, you could
lose your job as well.

You may want to alter the dates of a job you held to cover
a gap of unemployment, but what happens when you are
asked to talk about your employment history in an interview?
What if you become confused about what really happened and
what you wrote down? Furthermore, your prospective
employer is likely to verify some or all of the information on
your resume. A survey of human resources professionals by the
Society for Human Resource Management found that approxi-
mately 80 percent of respondents regularly verify the former
employers and length of service of job applicants. Additionally,
60 percent of respondents reported that they regularly confirm
previous job titles with former employers.

Save yourself from embarrassment and stick with the
truth. You will have no regrets if you do.

Introduce Yourself

A resume with a cover letter is one way you are able to introduce yourself to a prospective employer. You want to do everything you can to make sure your resume is reviewed and that it
successfully communicates who you are. There are no guaran-
tees it will be read, but there are things you can do to increase
the likelihood that it will be.

*Fourteen percent
of professionals
surveyed by
Vault.com admit
to lying on their
resumes. Twenty
percent claimed to
have "fudged a few
things, but nothing
I would consider a
lie." A majority of
respondents, 54
percent, said they
did not lie on their
resumes because "I
don't need to lie."*

*Vault.com workplace poll,
February 28, 2001*

What do you think an employer wants to hear? What will motivate someone to call you in for an interview? As you create your resume and cover letter, focus on the employer and his or her needs, interests, and priorities rather than your own.

Cover Your Bases with a Cover Letter

One way to add a personal touch when submitting your resume is by including a cover letter. This letter differs from a resume as it is written to the person doing the hiring and will most likely be read before he or she takes a look at your resume. Although some people feel a cover letter is optional, many experts advise applicants never to submit a resume without one.

Because this document is a *letter,* it is important to treat it like any other letter you would write. A cover letter needs to be addressed to a specific person, be signed in ink, and follow the basic standards of a business letter. Each letter should be crafted for its reader, so do some investigating before writing it, and always submit the original copy.

A cover letter needs to be addressed to a specific person, be signed in ink, and should follow the basic standards of a business letter.

A cover letter can be more personal than a resume, but you don't want to stray too far from a traditional business letter.

Dr. Randall S. Hansen, an employment consultant and co-author of *Dynamic Cover Letters* (Ten Speed Press, 2001), reveals the three most common cover letter mistakes:

1. Not addressing a letter to a named individual.

In most situations, job seekers who go the extra mile can find the name of the person they need to write to for a job interview. Sexist salutations (i.e. Gentlemen, Dear Sir) should be avoided at all costs. Don't address letters by the title of the person either. Taking the time to find the name of the individual is much more effective.

2. Failing to be proactive by requesting an interview.

Job seekers need to take the initiative in cover letters and ask for the interview. You should only be writing the letter if you feel you are qualified for the position, so don't end the letter weakly by saying something like "I look forward to hearing from you." Instead, end the letter by saying something like "I will call you the week of October 3 to set up an interview."

Surprising Statistics on Cover Letters and Resumes

The *SHRM Survey on Cover Letters and Resumes* reports the following statistics:

- Sixty-seven percent of resumes received today by human resources (HR) departments are accompanied by a cover letter.

- More than 80 percent of HR professionals spend less than one minute reading a cover letter.

- 76 percent of HR professionals say that a typo or grammatical error on a cover letter would remove an applicant from consideration for a job.

- The majority of resumes are sent through mail (42 percent) or by fax (30 percent).

- Fewer than 20 percent of resumes are submitted by e-mail; surprisingly, more than 33 percent of survey respondents said that e-mail is their preferred delivery method for resumes.

Source: Society for Human Resource Management

3. Telling what the company can do for you rather than what you can do for the company.

Employers don't care that hiring you will fulfill one of your lifelong ambitions; instead, they want to know what you can do for them. Job seekers need to show potential employers that they can make an immediate impact on the job.

In addition, as with the resume, you want to make sure that your letter is error free and that you keep it brief.

The Right Words

In Chapter 1, you had the chance to think about the types of words that best describe who you are. Because a cover letter and resume are your introduction, you want to use words that will hopefully move the reader to action—by asking you for an interview.

Avoid wishful thinking, such as "I hope you will find my resume impressive." Make assertive, powerful statements such as "I am certain you will find that my experience and skills are a perfect match to the qualifications you seek for this position."

Don't be afraid to say, "I am an excellent candidate for this position and I look forward to meeting with you."

Always end your letter by thanking the person for their time and stating your next move as specifically as you can by saying, "I will call you on [name the date]," "I will contact you next week," or "You can expect to hear from me by [name the date]."

This shows that you are a person who will take charge and take the lead. If you say you will call on a certain day, be sure to do as you say. Nothing will discredit you faster than failing to follow through on your promises.

References

Once a company is interested in you, you probably will be asked to provide references. Usually, providing two or three references is sufficient. Always seek permission before using someone as a reference. You wouldn't want anyone to be shocked to receive a call and become tongue tied when answering questions about you.

Select your references carefully and select people from different areas of your life—family members are not recommended. Try to include someone you have worked for or with, someone who knows you personally, and someone who knows you academically.

You may want to ask a few people to write reference letters or letters of recommendation so that you can give them to a hiring manager if requested.

The Telephone is a Useful Tool

Once you've worked hard to create the perfect resume and have submitted it to a number of companies, you hope it will do its job and help you obtain interviews. So, you sit back and wait for a phone call. What if the phone doesn't ring? What will you do?

Hopefully, you will not wait too long. If you want to be noticed, do something to stand out. Make yourself visible by calling and letting people know who you are.

You can call to verify that your resume arrived safely, to inquire about the status of the position, or to reaffirm your interest in the position. It is best to talk directly with the decision maker when possible, but many times you will not get past an assistant. This is fine and the assistant may be able to provide you with valuable information about the company, the job that you applied for, and the pace of the interviewing process.

If you want to be noticed, do something to stand out. Make yourself visible by calling and letting people know who you are.

While you don't want to become a pest, you do need to take control of as much of the job-hunting process as you can. If you sense your calls are unwelcome, back off, but ask questions to help you determine how to proceed.

Keep in mind the following tips when you are faced with making a difficult call:

- Have a purpose for your call.
- State the purpose of your call.
- Begin with an appropriate salutation such as "good morning," "good afternoon," or "hello."
- Ask for someone by name when possible.
- Always introduce yourself by name.
- Speak in an enthusiastic and upbeat manner.
- Ask for help. Say: "Are you able to suggest a next step for me?" or "Do you have any suggestions as to how I might schedule an appointment for an interview?"
- Always thank someone for speaking with you.
- Leave a message with your name and number when possible.
- Develop an outline or script to follow prior to making calls and consider practicing what you want to say to help you become more comfortable.

Test Your Resume and Cover Letter Writing Skills

Questions and Answers

True, False, or Depends?

1.

In order to make your resume stand out from others, print it on brightly colored paper.

False. Resumes on colored paper will stand out, but not in a positive way. While colored paper, unique fonts, and an overly decorative design show off your creative side, when it comes to sorting through resumes, companies prefer the tried and true. However, if you are in a creative or artistic field, you certainly have more leeway. Stick with neutral colored paper; white, off-white, eggshell, or pale gray are some of the best and safest choices.

2.

A resume never should exceed one page.

Depends. It is best to fit all of your information on one page. A brief resume is preferred, but the length of your resume should be determined by the necessary information that will best sell you to the employer. The main goal is to send the right message and convey your qualifications. One to two pages is standard for a typical resume.

3.

It is not necessary to submit a cover letter with your resume.

False. A cover letter gives you an opportunity to introduce yourself with a personal touch. While your resume basically stays the same wherever you send it, cover letters can vary. A cover letter enables you to tailor your message to each position and company you send it to.

4.

It is fine to lie a little on your resume if it will help you get an interview.

False. Never lie, even a little, on your resume. You may be tempted to adjust dates or enhance your resume in order to make yourself look better, but doing this can backfire. You never know when a potential employer will do some digging and find the truth. In an interview, you may be asked to talk about something on your resume. It will be easier to tell the truth than try to remember what you wrote as a cover up.

Starting a job dishonestly creates future problems. What will happen if down the road the truth is uncovered and it is discovered that you lied? It could cost you your job. Honesty is always the best policy.

5.

It is best to submit your resume by e-mail.

Depends. A recent survey found that nearly half of the respondents preferred to receive resumes via e-mail. As e-mail is used more and more, that figure will likely grow. However, even when you submit your resume electronically, it is good to also send it by mail or hand deliver it.

6.

A resume should not be folded.

True. Your resume should be presented as nicely as possible. Use envelopes that enable you to send your resume without folding it.

7.

If you don't have access to a computer, you can hand write your resume as long as your handwriting is neat and legible.

False. If you want to compete with the other resumes, you have to be on par with the competition. Your competitors are using a computer and you should too. Computers and printers are generally available for use at school or public libraries, at a friend's house, or even for short-term rental. Find one to use to create and print your resume. The more professional looking your resume, the more professional you will look. Give yourself a fighting chance.

8.

To help personalize your resume, include a picture of yourself.

False. This works well on some business cards and sounds like a good idea but is not recommended. Your objectives may be misunderstood. Companies don't want to be manipulated by your race, age, or beauty. Show your face for the first time when you go to the interview.

9.

The more references you have, the better, so include as many as you can on your resume.

False. Sometimes less is more. It's not the number of references you have, it's the quality of them that counts. Two or three solid references will be sufficient. Remember, a resume needs to be brief, so don't waste precious space listing references. List the things an employer wants to see. Once you have an interview and the company is interested, you will most likely be asked for references. List your references on a separate sheet of paper (use paper that matches your resume) and provide them when requested.

10.

Don't call a potential employer after submitting a resume. You will be called if you are qualified for the position.

False. If you wait to get a call, it may never come. Hundreds of resumes can be received for one job opening. If you call, you have a better chance of being noticed and considered for an interview than if you don't. Take your job search into your own hands and make something happen.

Chapter Summary

✓ Take your time when preparing your resume. Spend enough time creating your resume to ensure it does its job, which is to get you noticed and obtain interviews. You want your resume to represent you well.

✓ Have someone critique and proofread your resume. Seek the advice of others when preparing your resume, and have several people proofread it before you submit a copy to anyone. Typos or mistakes will immediately disqualify you as a candidate for most positions.

✓ Keep your resume brief and reader friendly. Limit your resume to one page whenever possible. Use bullets, lists, and an easy-to-read font, point size, style, and format.

✓ Send your resume by e-mail and by regular mail. Whenever possible, deliver your resume in person. Never fold, staple, or tape your resume. Use neutral colored paper and make sure your resume is free of stains and marks.

✓ Write a cover letter addressed directly to the hiring person and include it with your resume. This will enable you to personalize yourself and your resume, and will give you an advantage over those who omit this step.

✓ Speak affirmatively. Never use words such as "hope" or "wish." Assert yourself and let a potential employer know that you know you can do the job. Rather than asking for an interview, request one. Always state your intentions and objectives.

✓ Follow up with a telephone call. Make a call to ensure your resume arrived, to check the status of the position, or to ask for an interview. Befriend assistants or anyone you talk with and don't be afraid to ask for help. The telephone can be your best tool if you use it wisely.

✓ Make yourself available. Include telephone numbers and an e-mail address in all of your communication. Make it easy for an employer to reach you, especially during business hours. Be available to talk on the phone or to attend an interview. If it becomes too challenging for an interested employer to reach you, he or she may become irritated or just move on to someone else.

Chapter 3

Interview Dos and Don'ts

Test Your Interview Competence

True or False?

1.

If an interviewer addresses you by your first name, it's fine for you to do the same.

2.

A thank you note should be written immediately after the interview.

3.

If you are told that the company is a "casual" company, you can assume it is fine for you to dress casually for the interview.

4.

Arrive early, but not too early, for an interview.

5.

If you smoke cigarettes, spray cologne on yourself before the interview to help mask the smell.

6.

If you are nervous, chewing gum will help calm you.

7.

When deciding what to wear, select the nicest clothing you own.

8.

In most situations, the decision to hire someone is made within the first few minutes of an interview.

9.

If you are offered a beverage before or during the interview, accept it.

10.

When entering an office, select the chair that looks the most comfortable and sit down right away.

11.

Laughing a lot shows that you have a good sense of humor.

12.

Don't ask questions unless you are asked if you have any.

Test yourself as you read through this chapter. The answers appear on pages 81-84.

Creating Your Winning Impression

You've invested a lot of time creating the perfect resume. When you receive a call for an interview, you'll know that your hard work has paid off and that your resume has represented you sufficiently to proceed to the next level of your job search. A request for an interview indicates that you have passed the criteria necessary to warrant a face-to-face meeting and that someone is interested in learning more about you. Now that you have an interview scheduled, how much time should you spend preparing for this important next step?

For some reason, many people fail to properly plan for an interview and inaccurately assume that once they validate their credentials they will receive a job offer. Unfortunately, it isn't that simple. Planning for an interview is crucial, because the impression you make when you walk through the door has the potential to qualify or disqualify you for the job you are seeking within moments.

Although many interviewers don't like to admit that they make judgments so quickly about job candidates, the reality is that most do. The initial glance and a handshake are about all it takes for someone to think they have a sense of who you are. People who are adept at interviewing develop an ability to see beyond the first impression, but many do not because the first impression is so telling.

If you fail to make a good impression, you decrease your chances for a second interview and your chances for a job offer. There are many individuals who have credentials equivalent to yours. If an employer has a number of candidates to choose from, he or she needs to find an easy and quick way to distinguish one candidate from another. Sometimes an interviewer will rely on his or her first impression or gut feeling about a job candidate and make a decision within moments of meeting you.

So how much time do you think you have to make a winning impression? Hours? Minutes? Seconds?

Why You Never Have a Second Chance to Make a First Impression

Have you ever met anyone you connected with instantly? Have you ever met anyone you knew you didn't like even though

Planning for an interview is crucial, because the impression you make when you walk through the door has the potential to qualify or disqualify you for the job you are seeking within moments.

there was no concrete reason for your feelings? Most of us make decisions about others very quickly, unfairly, and sometimes inaccurately. Making a good impression isn't something that just happens to you. If you want to create a positive impression, you need to have a plan and then implement it within the first *10 seconds* of meeting someone.

Ten seconds is all it takes for someone to formulate initial, but long lasting, assumptions about you. An impressive resume will not overcome your unsuitable attire, weak handshake, or inappropriate comment made in the critical moments of initial judgment. In fact, the initial judgments are so long lasting that if you make a negative impression you will have to work awfully hard at changing the other person's opinion of you. And, no matter how hard you try, you may not be able to do it.

Have you ever misjudged someone? Several years ago I met a woman I would be working with on a project, and I was unimpressed. She was dressed much differently than I expected for someone of her status. Her hair needed to be combed and styled, she was sloppy in her appearance, and she had a sarcastic comment to say about everything. I was not looking forward to working with her but needed to due to the project we were both working on.

As time went on and I got to know her better, I learned that she was pregnant (with her fifth child) and found out that on the day I met her she hadn't been feeling well due to morning sickness. That explained her appearance. I began to appreciate and understand her sarcasm and, after getting to know her better, found her to be a wonderful and talented person. I was happy to admit that I had been wrong in my initial assumptions about her, but I was never able to forget the way I viewed her initially.

To this day, I feel guilty when I think about how I misjudged her. I am glad we were forced to work together and that I had the opportunity to discover more about her. It would be nice if there were enough time to get to know everyone we meet, but we don't, so we rely on instant impressions instead.

You never have a second chance to make a first impression. In an interview, you may never be considered for a position if you don't make the *right* impression the first time.

If you fail to make a good impression, you decrease your chances for a second interview and your chances for a job offer.

After the First Impression

Hopefully, you will make a favorable first impression. This provides you with the opportunity to "sell" yourself for the remainder of the interview.

A recent survey developed by Accountemps, a temporary staffing service, asked executives of the nation's 1,000 largest companies this question: How many minutes into an interview do you know whether or not a candidate is a fit for the job?

The mean response was 16 minutes!

"Applicants must be able to present a summary of their qualifications in a concise, enthusiastic, and poised manner, or they may lose their relatively short window of opportunity," says Max Messmer, chairman of Accountemps. "During the initial minutes of an interview, managers will be assessing whether candidates should move to the next step in their hiring processes, which may include additional interviews and skills tests as well as having references verified."

To help make a positive impression in the first few minutes, Messmer stresses the importance of thorough preparation prior to an interview. Anticipating and being ready to answer questions likely to come up at the beginning of a meeting is helpful.

Many interviewers begin an interview by saying, "Tell me a little about yourself." Don't wait until you are in an interview to decide what your response will be. Anticipate the question and have an answer prepared. Other questions commonly asked include "What are your greatest strengths or outstanding qualities?" "How do you react under pressure?" "Why should I hire you?" and "What are your weaknesses?"

You never have a second chance to make a first impression.

Prepare short and concise answers to these and other questions likely to be asked. Whatever you do, be honest and speak the truth. The more prepared you are, the better you will do in the interview and the better you will fare overall.

How We Communicate

Many years ago, a study conducted by Dr. Albert Mehrabian, of the University of California, Los Angeles, found that the way we appear and the manner in which we say something overshadows the content of our conversation.

In my seminars, I often ask participants what percent of our communication comes from the words we speak. What do you think: 25 or 50 percent? Most people think it is higher than it really is. We work hard at finding the perfect words, and speaking as accurately as possible.

According to Dr. Mehrabian's study, we communicate through the following ways:

- Body language sends 55% of our message.
- Tone of voice sends 38% of our message.
- Words send 7% of our message.

This indicates that only 7 percent of your overall message comes from the words you use. *What* you say is not nearly as influential or important as *how* you say it.

Have you ever been misunderstood? What happened? Perhaps you intended to communicate something but didn't get your point across successfully. Sometimes we are not congruent in our communication; our body language and tone of voice may contradict our words.

Your resume represents you. If it represents you in the correct way for a particular position, you will be called for an interview. When you meet a prospective employer for the first time, will you appear in a way that reinforces and surpasses that person's expectations, or will you be somewhat of a disappointment?

You may hope to meet and exceed an employer's expectation, but hoping won't make it happen. The manner in which you present yourself is up to you, but remember, you need to communicate who you are within the first few *seconds*.

> What *you say is not nearly as influential or important as* how *you say it.*

Understanding the Way Your Body Talks

From the moment you are born, you communicate with your body. What is more endearing than a baby's smile? Or feeling a baby grasp onto your finger? Smiling, touching, cooing, and crying are the only ways babies know how to communicate. Until we develop a working vocabulary, we communicate with our eyes, our cries, and our sighs.

We never lose the ability to communicate with our bodies (non-verbally), but as we get older we rely more and more on words and have a tendency to forget about our nonverbal messages.

I remember the time my daughter Samantha made up a story so that she wouldn't get into trouble. She had a few friends sleep over, and they snuck out of the house in the middle of the night to tee-pee another friend's house in the neighborhood. I wouldn't have known about it if I hadn't found the toilet paper wrappers under her sleeping bag. When I questioned her, Samantha denied everything. She came up with a number of reasons as to why the wrappers were under her sleeping bag. I wanted to believe her and I almost bought into her stories, but her body language gave her away. Just by looking at her, it was obvious she was not telling the truth. Samantha wouldn't look me in the eyes, she held her head low, and when I asked her if she was lying, she said no, but smiled as she said it.

Don't even think about telling a lie in an interview. Not only will a lie catch up with you eventually, it is very likely that you will give it away nonverbally. We may be able to mask our words, but it is far more difficult to mask our emotions.

My oldest daughter, Stephanie, dislikes speaking before a group because her face turns red as soon as she starts talking. Giving the speech doesn't bother her nearly as much as knowing her face is bright red. She knows that even if she sounds okay, people will notice her red face.

Your body speaks volumes about you and has a language of its own. The way you stand, sit, walk, tilt your head, fold your hands, cross your arms, and even the manner in which you blink speaks louder than your words. Your body language will either reinforce or contradict what you say. You can use this to your advantage as long as you remain aware and in control of the language your body speaks.

Don't even think about telling a lie in an interview. Not only will a lie catch up with you eventually, it is very likely that you will give it away nonverbally.

Ingredients of a First Impression

When you meet someone, within a matter of seconds and without saying a word, you are communicating. You *speak* both verbally and nonverbally. Following are the ingredients of a first impression:

Verbal	Nonverbal
(45% of communication)	(55% of communication)
Tone of voice	Appearance
Choice of words	Clothing
Rate of speech	Gesture
Enunciation	Posture
Volume of speech	Expressions
Attitude	Eyes

How to Make a Great Impression in 10 Seconds or Less

All it takes to make a great impression is to identify the kind of impression you want to make and create a plan to carry it through. Most people want to make a good impression but fail to figure out how to make it happen. Making a positive impression starts with awareness of yourself and others. And because everything is noticed and evaluated, you need to think about many things in order to send the right message.

Let's look again at the ingredients of a first impression, but this time I will review what you can do in each area to capture the image you want to make a positive impression.

Tone of Voice

Have you ever sensed that someone was upset, yet when you asked if everything was okay, the person replied, "I'm FINE" in a tone that contradicted their words? The manner in which you speak validates or invalidates what you say. Your tone also has the ability to add interest to the words you use. When you greet someone and you say, "It's nice to meet you," do you sound sincere and truly happy to meet that person or does your tone and pitch detract from your sincerity?

Suggestion: Speak enthusiastically and make sure your tone matches your words.

Choice of Words

The words you use enable you to express what you are thinking and to build rapport with others. Swearing, for example, is obviously perceived negatively. In a business environment, people expect you to have a command of the English language and to use a business vocabulary. This doesn't mean you have to necessarily learn new words, but if a large part of your vocabulary is full of slang or jargon, you will sound as though you do not belong in a business environment. In addition, many people use fillers in their conversations by overusing "ums," "ahs," and "ers" in between words. A few fillers aren't usually noticed, but if you use them too often, it will be the *only* thing noticed.

Suggestion: Work on building your vocabulary and avoid swearing and using slang, jargon, and fillers.

Rate of Speech

When I was young, I had a friend named Debbie who talked so fast that it was sometimes difficult to understand her. In fact, my mom always knew who was calling when Debbie was on the phone because she spoke so rapidly. Personally, I prefer fast talkers to slow talkers, but both types can be difficult to listen to. Talking too fast or too slow can make you appear nervous. Notice the rate of newscasters and other people you find easy to listen to and work to match that pace.

Talking too fast or too slow can make you appear nervous.

Suggestion: If you tend to talk fast, slow down, and if you tend to speak too slow, speed up.

Enunciation

If you want people to understand you, you need to speak clearly. I used to go to a doctor who mumbled. He was intelligent and a fine human being, but I couldn't understand half of what he said. I felt funny asking him for clarification repeatedly, and I know I missed some of the information I needed. I am certain that better communication skills would have improved his effectiveness.

Suggestion: Listen to yourself on a tape recorder for an accurate appraisal of your enunciation and speech habits.

Volume of Speech

My family tends to have very interactive and loud dinner conversations. We interrupt each other and, in order to be heard, we turn up the volume (or vocal chords). When we are out in public, we have to remember to talk quietly so we won't bother others. I have a tendency to project my voice loudly, which works very well when I am speaking to a large group. But when I am having a more personal conversation, I need to remember to speak more quietly. If you are too loud, you can appear rude. If you are too quiet, you risk appearing timid. Err on the side of loudness over quietness, but don't speak much louder than the person you are in conversation with.

Suggestion: Speak confidently and enthusiastically and try to match the volume of the person you are with, but don't be too boisterous.

Attitude

It only takes a quick glance at someone to determine his or her attitude. Your attitude is visible through the way you present your-self. If you are enthused, it shows. If you are nervous, it too shows—unless you make the decision to project confidence.

If you are too loud, you can appear rude. If you are too quiet, you risk appearing timid.

A positive, confident, and enthusiastic attitude helps you make a great impression, and these qualities come from within. Even if you don't feel confident or enthusiastic, act as though you do. It may feel phony at first, but you will be surprised to discover that the way you act affects the way you feel. Abraham Lincoln once said, "People are just about as happy as they make their minds up to be." Make up your mind to have a pos-itive and enthusiastic attitude.

Whatever you do, speak positively about yourself and never complain about past experiences or other people. Don't be full of doom and gloom—be a spark of positive energy. Be a good listener and a good conversationalist, but don't talk too much or monopolize the conversation.

Suggestion: Develop an optimistic mind-set and an upbeat attitude and you will have an advantage over those who are self-doubting.

Appearance

I was taking a class and noticed that the presenter was wearing a jacket that was at least two sizes too big. In addition, she was in desperate need of a haircut. Her appearance was distracting, and although she had knowledge about the subject she was teaching, her untidy image caused me to question her credibil-ity and level of success.

Make sure your clothing fits and is in good condition. Pay attention to detail and be well groomed. Jewelry should be simple and worn in small quantities. Cover tattoos if possible and make sure you're appearance is appropriate for the industry and position you are interviewing for. (Much more on appearance in Chapter 6.)

Suggestion: Take your appearance seriously and consider seeking the opinion of a cosmetics sales clerk, image consultant, hairstylist, or tailor before venturing out for an interview.

Clothing

"What should I wear?" is an important question to ask yourself when preparing for an interview. Go for the expected over the unexpected, the usual over the unusual, and dress a little better than is necessary. A suit is a safe bet. Don't worry about being overdressed. You are better off slightly overdressed than underdressed. (There will be more about what to wear to an interview later in this chapter.)

Suggestion: Buy a nice suit to wear to your interviews. It is your safest bet, even in a casual environment.

Make sure your clothing fits and is in good condition. Pay attention to detail and be well groomed.

Gestures

Although you may try to maintain control of yourself by restraining your gestures, don't restrict yourself too much. Gestures are a natural means of expression and help us animate our conversations. Strong, bold gestures add impact to what we say, while smaller gestures tend to reflect nervousness or anxiety. One of the most powerful gestures is the steeple, which is created by holding your hands together with fingers straight and pointing up. It is considered a position of power as long as the hands are above the waist and pointing upward.

Suggestion: Find a "home base" (your lap, a table, or a desk) to place your hands when you don't know what to do with them, but feel free to use your hands as you are talking or to emphasize a point.

Posture

You don't want to slouch, but don't be too rigid, either. Slouching conveys a lack of confidence, laziness, or even bore-

Gestures to Avoid

✗ **Pointing.** You may give the impression you are reprimanding someone or appear too aggressive.

✗ **Hands covering your mouth.** People may think you are uncomfortable, lying, or covering up something—literally, like the truth.

✗ **Rubbing or stroking body parts.** Rubbing yourself could appear as though you are trying to comfort or reassure yourself.

✗ **Playing and fiddling with jewelry, tapping a pencil, and swinging your leg.** These actions convey nervousness and uneasiness.

✗ **Hands in pockets.** You could be perceived as closed, unapproachable, or uneasy; add jingling the change in your pocket and you risk appearing nervous or uncomfortable.

✗ **Hands on hips.** This can convey defensiveness.

✗ **Crossed/folded arms on chest.** It may look like you are protecting yourself, and you risk appearing close-minded or unapproachable.

dom. If you are too rigid, you risk appearing uncomfortable, too formal, or unapproachable.

Always rise when you greet someone, and stand erect, with your shoulders back and head held high. Walk with a confident stride to convey a sense of direction, energy, and purpose.

Don't rush into the office and sit in the most comfortable-looking spot. Wait until you are invited to sit down. When you are seated, sit upright with your feet touching the ground. If you have a choice between a hardback chair and a soft cushiony chair, choose the hardback. You will be in a better position to maintain good posture.

Suggestion: In order to greet people confidently, stand tall with your head held high and walk with a brisk confident stride.

Expression

Are you aware of the expression on your face right now? You may be engrossed in this book, but if someone else were to see you, you might appear bored or even upset. It is important to vary your facial expressions in order to avoid being misread. Perhaps you've heard the expression "A smile is worth a thousand words." A smile conveys friendliness in any language and is a wonderful business tool. Smiling helps you come across as friendly, approachable, and confident.

A smile conveys friendliness in any language and is a wonderful business tool.

Do you look at the person you are talking to? Eye contact is essential in building trust and should be maintained as much as 90 percent of the time when talking with someone. When you fail to make eye contact you risk appearing disinterested, dishonest, or unsure of yourself. If you are uncomfortable looking someone in the eyes, focus on some other feature on their face, such as the bridge of their nose.

Suggestion: Smile as you say, "Hello, it's nice to meet you." Be aware of the expression on your face and make a connection with your eyes.

How to Impress When You're Under Duress

Most people experience some nervousness before an interview. Don't let your apprehension get the best of you. Even seasoned performers experience some nervousness before a performance, which can actually help to stimulate a great performance. As one actress said, "Either I suffer, or my work does."

Hall of Fame basketball player Bill Russell became sick before every game he played. His teammates claimed that the sicker he got, the better he played. You don't need to become ill before an interview to do well; the key is to use you nervousness to your advantage. Turn it into positive energy and excitement.

The only way you will feel excited and reduce the amount of nervousness you experience is by coming to an interview fully prepared. There is plenty of easily accessible information available to help you gear up for this important event.

As one employer stated: "I was always taught never to go into an interview without knowing something about the com-

The 15 Most Annoying Habits of Unsuccessful People

Through his research, Dr. James Bender, a New York psychologist, uncovered 15 of the most annoying gestures and irritating habits:

✗ Continuous blinking of the eyelids

✗ Nose picking or constant rubbing

✗ Twitching the eyebrows

✗ Cracking the knuckles

✗ Biting the lips

✗ Scratching the head

✗ Shrugging shoulders

✗ Smacking the lips

✗ Protruding the tongue

✗ Licking the lips

✗ Jerking the lips

✗ Pulling the ears

✗ Tapping the floor with a foot

✗ Swinging a crossed leg

✗ Finger tapping

We all need to blink, and it often isn't noticed when we do. However, blinking continuously and repeatedly becomes noticeable and potentially irritating to others. Any of these actions are acceptable if done in moderation, but when an action is repeated five or more times, it is more likely to be noticed.

pany. Nowadays, four out of five applicants who are asked, 'What do you know about our company?' expect me to tell them rather than research on their own. And it would be so easy for them to do these days, with most companies having a Web site or at least being mentioned on the Web somewhere! It seems to me to just be common courtesy and common sense to know something about the company that you want to work at."

Find out as much as possible about the company you are interviewing with prior to the interview. Do research on the Internet, visit the company's Web site, request company brochures, and learn about the industry by reading trade publications and other materials. Talk and network with others in the industry.

In addition to this book, read other books on interviewing. Ask a friend, parent, teacher, or career counselor to help you prepare for your interview. Have someone ask you questions so that you can practice and receive feedback on your answers. Know what is on your resume and be prepared to talk about any aspect of it. This may sound like common sense; it isn't. One person who does a lot of interviewing told me he always starts out an interview by asking the candidate to tell him about his or her resume. You need to know dates and the chronological sequence of events.

Come prepared with unique and intelligent questions specifically geared to the particular company and industry you are interviewing with. Martin Yate, author of the Knock 'Em Dead book series, says "People respect what you inspect, not what you expect." It is fine to inquire about the interviewer—what he or she likes about the company and how long he or she has worked there. Ask for a job description, about opportunities for growth and advancement, and about the company's competition.

If possible, travel to the location of the interview the day before so you can gauge the time it will take to get there and to ensure you won't get lost. Your preparation will reduce some of your stress, and as a result, you will improve your chances for a successful interview.

Anticipate some nervousness, but don't let it consume you. If you are prepared, you really don't have anything to be nervous about it.

If possible, travel to the location of the interview the day before so you can gauge the time it will take to get there and to ensure you won't get lost.

Influencing Potential Employers

A study conducted by the National Association of Colleges and Employers (NACE) provided employers with a list of 10 physical attributes and asked them to indicate the level of influence each would have on their opinion of a candidate's suitability for employment.

"A candidate's overall appearance is most likely to give a potential employer pause," says Marilyn Mackes, executive director of NACE. Grooming earned a 2.6 rating on a 3-point scale (where 1 = no influence, 2 = slight influence, and 3 = strong influence.)

Employers also rated the following:

- Nontraditional interview attire (2.3)
- Handshake (2.1)
- Nontraditional hair color (2.0)
- Obvious tattoos (2.0)
- Body piercing (2.0)
- Unusual hairstyle (1.9)
- Earrings on male recruits (1.6)
- Beard (1.2)
- Mustache (1.1)

No matter how little importance you place on your appearance, when you are looking for a job, appearance *does* matter. So do your handshake and attention to detail. It may seem as though this leaves you little room for individuality, but nothing could be further from the truth. You can be who you are and still present yourself professionally. Keep in mind that what you feel is a distinctive trait (for example, the ring in your nose, unusual tattoo, or unique hair color) could be the one and only thing that gets in the way of a prospective employer viewing you as a viable candidate for a job.

An interviewer is *looking* for reasons to eliminate you as a prospect. Why take a chance on anything that might diminish your chances of having a successful interview?

The Handshake

If you are male, you may have been taught to "shake like a man," but do you shake like a man with a woman, too? If you are a woman, do you shake hands at all? The handshake has been greatly underestimated and misunderstood. When you shake hands with someone (and you should whenever you meet someone male or female), the handshake provides you with additional information that you wouldn't have without adding the element of physical contact. The only appropriate time to touch someone in a business environment is when shaking hands.

Handshakes originated in ancient times as a gesture of peace. By offering a handshake, it showed that no weapon was concealed. Today, a handshake can set the tone of an interac-

You can be who you are and still present yourself professionally.

tion. When shaking hands, grasp the entire hand firmly, give a light squeeze, shake or pump once or twice, and let go.

I find that my handshake lasts longer if I am talking with a person as I shake their hand. However, if I introduce myself and then offer my hand, I can easily give one to two pumps and be done with the shake.

You don't want to make too strong of a statement by what you wear.

Many men are afraid of crushing a woman's hand. Women's hands are not that fragile. Avoid crushing someone's hand, but do shake firmly and strongly. A firm grip exudes friendliness and confidence. Practice and ask for feedback from others about your handshake.

How to Dress for an Interview

You've dressed up your resume, now you need to dress yourself up for the interview. Deciding what to wear often is a difficult decision to make. Many people have what they refer to as their "interview" outfit: the one outfit that is worn to every interview. This is fine, as long as it is appropriate and you feel good wearing it.

A conservative navy suit used to be the norm for interview apparel and was considered an interview uniform. Navy blue still is a neutral and safe color, but it is no longer the epitome of business dress. Every industry dictates its own dress code. To help you determine what to wear, ask yourself the following questions:

Is the industry I am focusing on conservative and traditional or is it unconventional and trendy?

If it is a traditional industry and generally conservative, then you want to dress conservatively. Neutral colors and classic styles in a suit are your best choice. If the industry is high tech or creative, you have more options when deciding what to wear. Brighter colors and trendier styles are more acceptable. Although a suit can still be worn, you have more latitude when you make your selection. You don't want to make too strong of a statement by what you wear. Avoid strong patterns, prints, or unusual colors.

What is the dress code at the company I am interviewing with?

Find out the dress code by talking with someone at the company. If you don't know anyone who works there, call and talk with a receptionist or someone who can give you this information. If it is a casual environment, you have more leeway in your clothing selection. But even if the company has a casual dress policy, you are not a part of the company yet, so you don't want to dress too casually.

Where is the company located?

Is it in a business district, downtown, or in a warehouse? The location also helps you determine the culture of the organization. If you have a chance, visit the company ahead of time and observe. Notice what people are wearing.

How long has the company been around?

Is this a new growing company or an established firm? Established firms tend to be more conservative than the young, up-and-coming organizations.

Who will I be interviewing with?

Is your interview with a human resource director, sales manager, or CEO? The title and rank of the person you will be meeting with can make a difference in your preparation. Find out whatever you can about the person you will be talking with to help you present the best image.

Although the answers to these questions will help you identify what the company might expect of you, you are still better off if you choose to be more conservative than avant-garde.

The casual environment that so many companies have adopted has caused a lot of confusion for many employees. Even people who work in a casual environment often wonder about what to wear. If you are interviewing with a company that has a casual dress code, you will probably see people dressed in a variety of styles and degrees of casual. In part, this is because in many companies casual has not been clearly defined.

Sometimes a job candidate is told that the company is casual and assumes that this is an invitation to dress more casually. This doesn't mean you should. When nothing is said about dress codes, it is up to you to decide what type of clothing to wear. Keep in mind that there probably are others who are interviewing for the same position who have also thought about what to wear. If you decide to dress more casually than job candidates who dress more formally, you risk appearing indifferent.

Dressing up for an interview is expected. You and the employer know that you are under scrutiny. Why do anything that might reflect negatively on you? This is your moment to shine and put your best foot forward. A suit is a safe selection and always communicates professionalism as long as it is an up-to-date style and fits you well. Pay attention to detail, or better yet, pay a visit to a tailor for a detail check.

Is That What You're Wearing?

Here are some of your best bets for interview attire. They are listed in order of formality, from the most professional choices to the more casual choices.

Women:
> Matching skirted suit (first best choice)
> Matching pantsuit (second best choice)
> Jacket with a skirt
> Jacket with a dress
> Jacket with slacks

Men:
> Matching suit (best choice)
> Blazer with slacks
> Sport coat with slacks
> Shirt with tie and slacks
> Sweater with slacks

Of the many choices, the matching two-piece suit is your best choice for interview attire. Although I listed a couple of options for men that do not include a jacket, I recommend wearing a jacket for an interview, even in a casual environment. However, if it is a high tech or very casual environment and you are on your second or third interview and have been invited to dress more casually, then the other options apply. A jacket always adds a touch of professionalism and sense of completion to anything you wear. Don't, however, remove your jacket during an interview unless you are encouraged to take it off.

You want to make a great impression, and showing that you dressed up for the interview displays your respect for the person you will be with. Make sure your clothing is clean, well pressed, and in good condition.

Attention to Detail

Hands and Nails

During the interview, you will be evaluated on a number of things, including your attention to detail. For example, your hands and nails will be noticed. People who have claw-like nails or unusually bright colors or fancy artwork on their nails draw too much attention to their hands, and the perception can be negative. If you've spent the previous day house cleaning or gardening, clean your nails so that you don't show up with dirt under your nails. Well-groomed, manicured hands are important, male or female.

Shoes: Put Your Best Foot Forward

Pay attention to the condition of your shoes. People who do a lot of interviewing often wait until the end of the interview to check out the condition of the applicant's shoes. If they are scuffed and the heels are worn down, it will be noticed. Shoes in poor condition reflect poorly on you. You need to be well dressed from head to toe—literally. Take the time to polish your shoes and make sure they are in good condition. It shows that you pay attention to detail—something employers look for in a job candidate.

Tattoos and Body Piercing

Tattoos and body piercing have the potential to be viewed negatively, especially in a more conservative work environment. If you have anything other than pierced ears, remove the earring(s). If you have more than two or three holes in your ears, take out some of the earrings. Although pierced ears on men have gained in popularity and are more acceptable in general, they aren't necessarily an established or conventional business look. If you are male, I recommend taking out your earring(s). Why flaunt anything that has the potential to distract from your talent, qualifications, and ability?

Facial Hair

Men who have facial hair should have it trimmed close to the face. Long, shaggy beards and mustaches can make you appear unkempt. Mustaches are less risky than beards, but either can be a potential deterrent in some business environments. A clean-shaven face can give you an advantage.

In an interview, the expected will fare better over the unexpected. Don't take risks with your appearance. Go with the norm and increase your chances of receiving a job offer. There are many ways to distinguish yourself from others without compromising your individuality.

Your Manners Are Showing

That Dreaded Ring

You've figured out how to make a good impression, you've done your homework and are ready for the interview. You have the right look; having the right body language will prepare you for whatever comes your way. You are in the middle of your interview and a phone begins to ring. You look around as you wonder who forgot to turn a cell phone off and suddenly realize that it's *your* phone ringing. Y*ou* forgot to turn off *your* phone. What would you do: answer it, ignore it, apologize, explain who called, or just turn it off?

To avoid such a situation, you might consider leaving your phone at home or in your car when you have an interview. However, if you feel the need to bring your phone in with you, make sure it is turned off before you walk into the interview. Few things are as inappropriate as having your phone ringing during an interview, and even worse is for you to answer it and engage in a conversation.

There are many ways to distinguish yourself from others without compromising your individuality.

Stay Awake

What if you didn't sleep well the previous night and find yourself getting sleepy during the interview? It has happened. People have dozed off during an interview—not a wise thing to do. Get plenty of rest, try not to yawn during an interview, and be as alert and perky as possible.

If You're Sick

What if you have a bad cold? Is it acceptable to bring a box of tissue and a bag of lozenges for your scratchy throat? I will never forget the time I had a meeting with a gentleman who was suffering from a terrible cold. It wasn't until I sat down and began talking with him that I realized how ill he was. Thick mucus drained from his nose, which he kept blowing throughout the meeting. I was repulsed, and after he shook my hand, I couldn't wait to leave and wash off the germs!

If you are sick, reschedule the interview. If you risk a coughing attack, then bring a lozenge with you, but it is much easier to talk without anything in your mouth. Take cold medicine if necessary so that you won't have to blow your nose, cough, or sneeze during the interview.

Manners will never go out of style and are an asset to anyone, especially in an interview.

What's Noticed

The society we live in has become more casual, and many people mistakenly assume that good manners are a thing of the past. Manners will never go out of style and are an asset to anyone, especially in an interview. Displaying good manners conveys that you are well-bred, respectful of others, and have the ability to blend with ease into a variety of environments.

Vault.com, a career content site, conducted a survey on interview manners. Employers were asked if they felt that manners had deteriorated in the interviewing and hiring process over the last two years.

Following are the results of the survey:
51% — Yes, they have
29% — Yes, a bit
17% — Not very much
3% — Not at all

Interviewers have to put up with a lot, but the survey shows that they do have their limits.

The following percent of employers would automatically reject otherwise qualified candidates who indulged in these behaviors:

95%   would disqualify for making a cell phone call
89%   for leaving before the interview is over
86%   for accepting a cell phone call
86%   for bringing a pet
85%   for removing shoes
77%   for exhibiting poor hygiene
76%   for asking for a cigarette break
74%   for using profanity
61%   for applying/reapplying lipstick
60%   for bringing a child
30%   for arriving 10 minutes or more late
27%   for taking longer than a 10-minute bathroom break
10%   for arriving 30 minutes or more early
 4%   for removing a jacket

An employer who participated in the survey related the following story: "A male stripped down to the buff in the parking lot in full view of hundreds of offices and changed into his interview suit. I received a dozen phone calls warning me that he was on his way to my office. I barely kept a straight face in the interview."

The lesson: From the moment you pull into the company's parking lot or enter the building where the company is located, you are being scrutinized. Assume eyes are on you, because they probably are. For starters, make sure your car is clean and in good condition. If you pull up and your car is rumbling or noisy, you may draw attention to yourself in the same way you would if you were dropped off at the door in a limousine. Neither would help you to make a very good first impression.

Everyone you encounter could influence your job potential. Smile, say hello, and extend yourself in a friendly manner to the doorperson, the receptionist, the secretary, and anyone you come into contact with. Treat everyone with respect. Many interviewers rely on their secretary's opinion of a job candidate, so make sure you make a good impression with *everyone*.

The Effective Exit

It is important for you to be able to recognize when the interview has come to an end. There will come a point in the interview when the momentum will slow down a bit. You may be asked if you have any more questions, and if you do not, it may be the beginning of the end of the interview. It may be less overt; the interviewer may begin to gather papers or close the folder with your information. He or she may simply stand up, signaling that it is time for you to leave.

When the time has come for you to exit, gracefully stand up, express your desire for the position, determine the next step (for example, Is there any additional information the interviewer needs? When is a decision anticipated? Would a follow up call be appropriate?), thank the interviewer for his or her time, extend your hand for a farewell handshake, and say good-bye.

This is not the time to throw in the question you forgot to ask or change your interview behavior. Your exit is just as important as your entrance.

Thank You Note

When you return home from the interview, it is essential that you write and mail a thank you note within one day, and the sooner you do it, the better. It doesn't take much time to write a thank you note, and it may be the determining factor that sets you apart from other candidates. Surprisingly, many people underestimate the value of a thank you note.

When you return home from the interview, it is essential that you write and mail a thank you note within one day.

You don't need to write a lengthy note, and there is some debate over whether typed or handwritten notes are preferred. A thank you note should not be sent by e-mail or fax.

You want to make sure your note will be read. Studies have shown that executives will open hand-addressed envelopes before opening computer-generated labels or typed envelopes.

Think about the mail you receive. What type of letters do you open first? If you are like most people, it's not the bills or direct mail sent your way, but anything that is hand addressed that you open first. Typically, we don't receive much handwritten correspondence anymore; therefore, it has greater appeal and is more personal. However, if you choose to hand write a thank

Thanks, But No Thanks

A thank you note shows that you understand protocol; it validates your interest in the position and demonstrates initiative. Vault.com asked employers what, if any, impact the thank you note had on a candidate's chances of getting hired:

36%   It always helps.

42%   It helps when deciding between two or more candidates.

22%   It does not matter.

Employers were then asked how often they receive thank you notes from candidates. Their responses were as follows:

0%   100% of the time

10%   75–99% of the time

26%   50–74% of the time

20%   25–49% of the time

36%   1–24% of the time

8%   Nobody sends thank you notes anymore.

you note, make sure your handwriting is legible, and always write it on either personal stationary or on a nice note card.

The purpose of the note is to thank the person for his or her time, and the opportunity to interview for the position and to express your interest in working for this company. Your thank you note should be short, to the point, and mailed within 24 hours.

To Call or Not to Call?

Whether or not you should follow up with a phone call will be based somewhat on the final conversation you had at the interview. If, when determining your next step, the interviewer specifically told you not to call, then don't. If, however, it was left open as to who will follow up with whom, or if nothing was said, you can and should follow up with a phone call within one week.

Continue to ask what the next step is and to follow up if encouraged to do so, but be careful not to become a pest. Really listen to what the interviewer is telling you.

Above all, try to talk with the person directly when you call and avoid leaving too many voice mail messages if at all possible. If you find it necessary to leave a message, know what you plan on saying before you call. There is nothing worse than a long and rambling conversation about nothing. It's a good idea to write out what you want to say, as long as you can say it without sounding as though you are reading it.

Interviewing can be a positive, enriching experience. You can learn a lot about yourself through the job-seeking process. Evaluate every interview and identify what went well and what you would like to improve upon. If you don't receive an offer, don't be too hard on yourself or take it personally. You will have many additional opportunities for interviews and you *will* receive a job offer. When you do, you will know that it was worth waiting for.

Test Your Interview Competence

Questions and Answers

True or False?

1.

If an interviewer addresses you by your first name, it's fine for you to do the same.

False. Start out using the interviewer's surname. It's better to start out more formally than it is for you to assume it is acceptable to be on a first-name basis. If the interviewer requests that you use his or her first name, then do so.

2.

A thank you note should be written immediately after the interview.

True. It is important to send a thank you note within one business day of an interview. If you want to be sure your note will be read, hand write it. Addressed mail is always opened before other mail. Just make sure your writing is legible!

3.

If you are told that the company is a "casual" company, you can assume it is fine for you to dress casually for the interview.

False. This is your one and only chance to make a good first impression. Even if everyone else at the company is dressed casually, you are not like everyone else. They are employed; you are not. You may be competing with a number of other candidates who felt it was important to dress up for their interviews. Are you willing to risk being remembered as the one who looked less professional than the others? It is always better to be overdressed than underdressed. And you never have a second chance to make a first impression. Make your first impression your best.

4.

Arrive early, but not too early, for an interview.

True. If you arrive too early (30 minutes or more), you risk appearing too eager for the job and it may seem as though you have nothing better to do with your time. Always arrive in plenty of time (10 to 15 minutes early is ideal) and never arrive exactly on time or even one minute late. Be prepared to allow extra time to find your way, park, stop at the restroom, and relax before you have your interview.

5.

If you smoke cigarettes, spray cologne on yourself before the interview to help mask the smell.

False. You definitely don't want to smell like cigarette smoke (a real turn-off for most people), but trying to mask it with cologne is a big mistake. The combination of cigarettes and cologne may be too much for many people's sense of smell. Many people have allergies or sensitivities to perfumes and cologne. The last thing you want to do is be the cause of the interviewer's sneezing, itching, or coughing. In addition, smells are often associated with memories—both good and bad. You don't want to waltz into an interview smelling like and reminding the interviewer of his or her "ex", do you? And never smoke during the interview.

6.

If you are nervous, chewing gum will help calm you.

False. Chewing gum is unprofessional, nervous or not. The more nervous you are, the louder you are likely to chomp on your gum. Do not eat, chew, or suck on anything during the interview.

7.

When deciding what to wear, select the nicest clothing you own.

False. Just because something is your finest doesn't make it appropriate to wear to a job interview. Some women own very expensive (and skimpy) eveningwear that they consider their nicest garment. It may be a fine choice for formal events, but it is inappropriate for the workplace. Stick with good quality and classic garments for your interview attire.

8.

In most situations, the decision to hire someone is made within the first few minutes of an interview.

True. From the moment you walk through the door, the interviewer is noticing everything about you and, within a few minutes, probably feels he or she has a sense as to whether or not you are the one for the position. It is unfortunate that many interviews continue long after the person has been disqualified from consideration.

9.

If you are offered a beverage before or during the interview, accept it.

True. It is fine to accept a beverage if you want one. But if it causes you to run to the restroom in the middle of the interview or you think you might spill it, decline the offer. Don't bring your own beverage in with you and, even if an alcoholic drink will help calm your nerves, never consume alcohol before or during an interview.

10.

When entering an office, select the chair that looks the most comfortable and sit down right away.

False. You aren't the one who should select the chair. You are in someone's office. Let that person indicate where you are to sit. If you are given a choice don't select the couch or cushiony chair. Select the one that will help you maintain good posture. And wait to be seated until the interviewer is seated.

11.

Laughing a lot shows that you have a good sense of humor.

False. Laughing a lot shows that you either have a nervous laugh or that you are so nervous you think everything is funny. If something is said that warrants a chuckle, give in, but don't giggle your way through the entire interview.

12.

Don't ask questions unless you are asked if you have any.

False. An interview should flow like any other conversation. Always have a few good questions prepared and ask them at the appropriate time. Asking questions shows you have initiative and interest in the company.

Chapter Summary

To Ensure Interview Success:

✓ **Do your homework.** Find out as much as you can about the company in advance.

✓ **Be prepared.** Arm yourself with a few questions to ask and practice a few answers to some of the most commonly asked questions.

✓ **Look good.** Wear a suit and pay attention to other appearance details; make sure your hair is clean and styled, your clothing clean and pressed, and your shoes shined.

✓ **Exude confidence.** Smile, hold your head high, shoulders back, and walk with vigor.

✓ **Radiate friendliness.** Greet everyone (including the receptionist) with warmth.

✓ **Be positive.** Do not talk badly about yourself, other people, or complain about anything.

✓ **Extend yourself.** Offer a firm, strong handshake at the beginning and the end of an interview.

✓ **Use eye contact.** Maintain eye contact during your interview, glancing away occasionally, but always remaining focused on the person you are talking with.

✓ **Gesture naturally.** Find a home base for your hands and let your gestures add interest to your conversation.

✓ **Display respect.** Don't use first names unless you are asked to, rise when you greet someone, and be a good listener.

✓ **Be mindful of good manners.** Turn off your cell phone and do not eat, chew gum, smoke, or wear fragrance.

✓ **Be gracious.** Thank the interviewer for his or her time and hand-write and mail a thank you note within one business day.

✓ **Follow-up call.** Place a follow-up call to the interviewer. Do not call back if the interviewer explicitly requests that you do not call. If the interviewer has not indicated future contact protocol at the end of the interview, call back within a week to continue the interview process.

Section II:

You've Landed a Job, Now What?

Chapter 4

Your
First Day
on the Job

Test Your Readiness for the World of Work

True or False?

1.

One of your employer's greatest fears is that he or she has made a mistake by hiring you.

2.

Introduce yourself to everyone in the office on your first day of work.

3.

Once you get a job, you don't need to put forth as much energy as you did in the job interview.

4.

Eye contact should be avoided when you first meet someone.

5.

Make sure you understand the expectations your employer has of you, and if unsure about something, ask for clarification.

6.

Repeating someone's name after an introduction will help you to remember it.

Test yourself as you read through this chapter. The answers appear on pages 107-109.

The First Day

Finally, the moment you've been waiting for has arrived. You are about to experience the first day of your first *real* job. Congratulations!

You may be under the assumption that all of the preparation, learning, studying, and test taking you've endured to get to this point is behind you now. Perhaps you feel fully prepared for what lies ahead. I hope you are, but as you begin your new job and jump-start your career, you are embarking on what is sure to be one of the largest learning curves you've had yet.

Your first day on the job may bring back memories of the way you used to feel on the first day of school. Each year there was something special about that first day: the anticipation of a new teacher, the hope of making new friends, and the ability to start over with a clean slate. As you prepare for your first day of work, you will enjoy a new beginning as well. You will meet many new people, enter into a new environment, and have a new schedule to follow.

On the first day and for the first few weeks at your new job, you will be in a learning mode. It may help to view your first job as an extension of your education. Be prepared to listen and ask questions. You may even feel inadequate at times. If so, don't worry; it's all a part of the learning process.

The last thing you want to do is to begin your new job with a know-it-all, overly confident attitude.

The Right Attitude

The last thing you want to do is to begin your new job with a know-it-all, overly confident attitude. Your attitude will be an asset as long as you have the right attitude.

A recent survey by Accountemps, a temporary staffing service, polled chief financial officers from some of the nation's top accounting firms and asked them to identify the most valued interpersonal skill in job candidates. Positive attitude was rated as the most important skill. A positive attitude is an asset in any job. It is easier to enjoy what you do when you have a positive attitude. A positive attitude will create a domino effect, positively impacting everyone you encounter.

I receive hundreds of letters each year from the readers of my workplace advice column. Many of the problems I hear about have to do with the challenges of working with negative or difficult coworkers. Negative people make life miserable for everyone. The person who is always complaining is difficult to be around day after day, and can eventually bring down the spirit of everyone they encounter. Negative people rarely see themselves as the problem and are quick to blame others for their unhappiness. One negative person can change the tone of an entire group of people.

The world is full of trouble and sadness. How refreshing it is to be around someone who is upbeat, energetic, and positive. Some of the most successful people in the world are successful because of their positive attitudes. You will draw people to you if you are a positive person, and you will push people away with negativity. It never hurts to try to look on the bright side of things, and you will enjoy life more if you are optimistic.

You will draw people to you if you are a positive person, and you will push people away with negativity.

You are young and new to the workplace. You are not yet burned out from years of work. Hopefully, you will bring a sense of exhilaration and anticipation to this new job that many of your older coworkers have lost over the years. If you are energized, don't stifle yourself; infuse everyone around you with that energy. You can be a breath of fresh air for your department or entire company.

For some reason, many people believe that their attitude is something they acquire inherently and that it is out of their control. Your disposition may be something you are born with, but your attitude is your choice. We cannot control much of what happens to us in life, but we can control our reaction to what happens.

Proactive vs. Reactive

Imagine you have a job interview with a company you really want to work for. This is a dream job: a great starting salary, good benefits, room for growth, and plenty of flexibility. On the morning of the interview, you take extra time to prepare and leave early to make sure you arrive on time.

You are driving along and suddenly realize you have a flat tire. You pull over and are about to react to what has happened. What do you think a typical reaction might be?

I've used this scenario in my seminars many times, and based on the responses from my seminar participants, the first reaction most people say they would have is anger. Most people say that they would get mad. Upon discovering the flat tire you might swear, yell, cry, pound on the steering wheel, or even get out of the car and kick the tire.

You may begin to experience feelings of despair and decide you are destined for bad luck. You might even come to the conclusion that the job wasn't meant to be and give up.

These are common reactions, but simply reacting won't do anything to alter the situation. So what choices do you have?

You can refuse to react by becoming proactive instead. You can say to yourself, "So what, *now* what?" "What will I do about the fact that my tire is flat and I need to arrive in 15 minutes or risk missing the interview?" What could you do to gain control of the situation?

You could make a telephone call (for a cab, a tow truck, or to the person you will be meeting with) and explain what has happened. One participant in a seminar said she would call ahead to explain what happened *and* have doughnuts and coffee sent to the office! Now that's proactive! You can take control of what happens rather than let what happens take control of you.

Choosing to Survive

Debbie

My friend Debbie was diagnosed with pancreatic cancer a year ago. Her family and friends were devastated because her prognosis was not good. In fact, the doctors didn't offer her much hope. But Debbie refused to accept the prognosis. Debbie is a young woman with young children and is determined to survive. While experimenting with treatments, she has continued to live her life optimistically, surrounding herself with positive people and pursuing all of her interests.

Recently I had the privilege of attending a celebration for her. Although Debbie is not cured or even in remission, she is doing amazingly well. If you met her, you would never know what she is going through. She is energetic (she walks 3 miles daily), keeps busy with friends, and is always smiling. Her husband shook his head as he said to me, "It has to be the power of the mind. There is no other explanation for how well she is doing."

Don

Don, an acquaintance of mine, became a quadriplegic shortly after graduating high school. He was out for a motorcycle ride, was hit by someone driving a car (who left the scene), and was thrown from his bike. His life changed forever.

When he learned that he would never walk again, Don began using drugs to numb the emotional pain. He really didn't care about living anymore. Fortunately, he received the help he needed to overcome his addiction and despair. He decided that he wanted to live. He learned to draw by holding a pencil in his mouth and began creating beautiful pictures and greeting cards.

Today, in addition to selling his artwork, Don speaks to children and teenagers, empowering them to stay away from drugs, and encouraging them to develop a "can-do" attitude. His presence and uplifting spirit is extremely powerful. I have had the good fortune of hearing Don speak on a number of occasions and can tell you that he is one of the most inspiring people I have ever met. He is married now and lives a full life, simply because he made the decision to thrive and survive.

Putting Things in Perspective

Felix

Positive people can be found everywhere. Sometimes they appear when you least expect it. A few years ago, I flew into Chicago on a cold and snowy evening. I was tired and hungry as a result of a long day and somewhat irritated because my flight had been delayed. Once I got into the cab, the driver, who was very talkative, introduced himself and tried to make conversation with me. I wasn't very receptive. I was tired and just wanted to be alone in my thoughts. But Felix persisted and was so pleasant that it was difficult for me to avoid engaging in a conversation with him. Suddenly I realized that talking with him might be just what I needed to make a shift in my attitude and that perhaps there was a reason I was in that particular cab with this driver.

I started to listen to Felix and asked him questions. He told me that he had escaped from Cuba to the United States over 15 years ago and that he had been desperate to leave his country. Felix lived in hiding for two months prior to his escape, which took place in the middle of a driving rainstorm. He made the trip on a homemade, one-person boat built out of old truck tires. He spent over a week on this boat on the ocean and came close to death, but was fortunate enough to be rescued and become a U.S. citizen. His love of this country, the family he has created, and the obstacles he has overcome moved me.

Some of the most difficult people and challenging situations provide us with the most insight about ourselves and educate us about life.

Felix had such a positive outlook on life and told me he believes that life is what we choose to make of it. Listening to his life story and talking with him was uplifting. My frustration over running behind schedule was put into perspective. I became a different (and better) person as a result of that cab ride. I was able to let go of my previous frustration because I connected with another human being. I had been willing to distance myself from him and retreat into my own little world. Instead, I met someone who made me feel good about being alive and living in the United States, which is something I must admit I fail to think about some days.

Perhaps you've heard the saying "When the teacher is ready, the student will appear." We are all students (of life) and everyone we meet has the ability to teach us something. Some of the most difficult people and challenging situations provide us with the most insight about ourselves and educate us about life.

A Bad Teacher

In her junior year of high school, my daughter Stephanie had a chemistry teacher who was in his final year of teaching. It was obvious that he was counting the days until he could retire. He no longer cared about his students or about doing a good job.

Stephanie loved school and was deeply affected by this teacher. After seeing other students humiliated for asking questions in class, she stopped participating in discussions. Some days she would purposely miss his class in order to avoid him. Although many parents and students complained about him and his unusual tactics, nothing could be done. He would soon be gone, but not soon enough.

Stephanie was upset and angry. She didn't do well in his class and blamed him for ruining her grade point average. At times, she would cry just thinking about her grades. She couldn't find any reason for this to have happened, but I could.

You will encounter many difficult people throughout your life. You can't avoid these types of people, but you can avoid becoming like them and giving up who you are in their presence. You have the power to choose whether you will become a victim or whether you will thrive and survive.

If Stephanie failed chemistry, only she would suffer. Although there was nothing that could be done about this teacher, I told my daughter that she *could* learn something from him and become a better person as a result.

I have been affected by my friend Debbie's illness, and as a result of what she is going through, I appreciate every day that I feel well. I am more compassionate toward people with disabilities as a result of knowing Don. I have more appreciation for the great opportunities that are available in this country as the result of meeting Felix. I am even more appreciative of the many great teachers my children have had after experiencing what a poor teacher is like.

Everyone we meet has the potential to influence us, and we have the potential to influence everyone we encounter. I have decided that I want to be a positive influence on the people I meet. I feel better physically and emotionally when I am positive, and I know I make other people happier, too. What kind of influence do you want to have on others? It's your choice, and a decision only you can make. Think about it.

All About Commitment and Relationships

Once you've accepted a position, hopefully, you will be excited about it. If you aren't, you may want to evaluate why you

You have the power to choose whether you will become a victim or whether you will thrive and survive.

accepted the job. Job satisfaction often is at its highest at the beginning of a job.

It may help to view your new job like a new relationship. Think about the variety of relationships you have. Which ones are most important to you and why? You probably have a number of casual relationships, people who are in your life that you consider friends, even though you don't spend much time with them. You probably have other, closer relationships with people who are more involved in your day-to-day existence. Perhaps you've seen a number of your relationships come and go. What is the reason that some have outlasted others? Chances are it has to do with the quality and importance of the relationship and your commitment to it.

By accepting a job, you have entered into a new relationship, and you have made a commitment.

By accepting a job, you have entered into a new relationship, and you have made a commitment. Commitment levels vary from person to person. Have you thought about the kind of commitment you are willing to make? The following questions will help you determine your level of commitment.

How would you respond to the following questions?

Once you've accepted a job, how long do you plan on staying with the company?

If you plan on working there for a year or more, chances are you will take the job more seriously than if you view it as a short-term position or a launching pad for something better. Max Messmer, author of Job Hunting for Dummies (Hungry Minds, 1999), advises professionals to consider the long-term implications of frequent job moves. Companies look for a pattern of stability in new hires in order to reduce the risk of turnover.

Are you satisfied with your decision to work at this company?

Did you take the first offer that came along or compromise what you really wanted because you needed a job? If you are not satisfied at the onset of a job, you may never be happy working there. If you are truly unhappy, admit you made a mistake and leave before investing (and wasting) too much time.

Do you plan on continuing your job search (even though you are employed) so that you can keep your options open?

If so, you may never really take this job seriously. If you never end your search and continue to look for something better, you may not be able to give this job a fair chance.

If you become disillusioned and discover that this job isn't everything you had hoped it would be, will you leave?

It's almost certain that at some point you will become disillusioned with your job. If you choose to leave a job every time this happens, you may find yourself job hopping more than you planned. Your reaction will depend upon your level of commitment to this job. Many problems can be overcome, but you have to be willing to stay around to work things out.

If you are concerned or upset about something, will you talk about it with the appropriate people or are you the type who will keep your feelings to yourself?

Your answer to this question probably has a lot to do with the way you were brought up and your comfort level in expressing yourself. As in any relationship, if you are upset about something but say nothing, you will accomplish nothing. It is important to address issues that arise and to be honest with yourself, your supervisor, and coworkers.

Are you looking to do your job as it's stated in your job description or are you willing to do whatever it takes to get the job done?

A detailed job description will help you understand what is expected of you. However, there are other expectations your employer has of you that are implied rather than written or spoken. Your employer assumes you will be punctual, honest, trustworthy, dedicated, and hardworking. If you are willing to do more than what is expected, you will get more than you expect.

Your employer assumes you will be punctual, honest, trustworthy, dedicated, and hardworking.

The Unwritten, Unspoken Expectations

As in any relationship, things will work out better if you know what you want this job to be like and have a clear understanding of what is expected of you. If you take this commitment lightly, you are less apt to take your job seriously and may become disillusioned when problems arise. Without a strong sense of commitment, you may be more likely to leave if things don't work out as you planned. On the other hand, if you enter this relationship with the understanding that you want to gain some solid experience, you will probably view each hurdle you encounter as less threatening or significant.

The very first career opportunity I had was when I was just 20 years old. After taking (and loving) the Dale Carnegie course in public speaking and human relations, I gained the confidence I needed to leave the University of Minnesota and pursue a career in sales. I applied for a number of sales jobs, but many employers were hesitant to hire me because I lacked experience. I did, however, get a break with Dale Carnegie and began selling for them. I was given a territory and literally knocked on people's doors in an attempt to spread the word and sell the programs.

This type of cold calling was very challenging. I was selling something intangible, which was not easy, and I was not having much success. I knew that I had much more to learn. I decided that if I could gain some solid experience, I would be able to find a job selling a tangible product in the future. My father stressed the importance of stability and suggested I make a commitment to stick with the job for a full year. After that time, he advised, I would be in a better position to decide if I wanted to stay or leave.

It was a challenging year, but I stuck with the job and gained valuable experience as a result. When I left Dale Carnegie, I went to work for a company that had told me the previous year they couldn't hire me without sales experience. Now that I had the experience, I went back to them and got the job. Patience and perseverance are qualities employers admire and are what enabled me to get the job I wanted.

Relationships require time, effort, and hard work. You and your employer have entered into a partnership, and both partners must make contributions to the relationship for it to work out. Both you and your employer have expectations of each other. Although you may not feel the need to discuss each and every expectation you have with your supervisor once you are employed, the fact is that they do exist.

You probably assume your employer will:
- Pay you.
- Pay you on time.
- Respect you.
- Offer benefits.
- Allow breaks during the day.
- Conduct reviews.
- Give pay raises.
- Provide a desk, computer, and other tools to help you do your job.

Your employer also has expectations of *you*. These expectations often are implied, not spoken.

Your employer is counting on you to:
- Work hard each business day.
- Arrive on time.
- Assert yourself and take initiative to get things done.
- Have a positive attitude.
- Communicate clearly.
- Get along with coworkers.
- Look good.
- Act professionally.
- Do what you say.
- Be dedicated to your job.
- Be dependable.
- Be honest and trustworthy.

How would you feel if your employer missed a pay period or failed to live up to any of your expectations? You probably would not be very happy. Even though your employer may never specifically tell you some of the things that are expected, it doesn't mean the expectations don't exist. It is important for you to think about and identify the expectations your employer may have of you and to make sure you live up to those standards.

When you are offered a job, you can assume that you have met most of the expectations your employer had for the person who would fill this position.

Recognizing the importance of the job interview, you probably took the time to consider how you would present yourself for this important event. You might have spent hours selecting just the right outfit and practicing your answers to interview questions. On the day of your interview, you most likely made sure that you left in plenty of time, allowed for traffic, and arrived early so as to make a good impression. You probably were careful to present yourself in the best possible manner during your job interview.

Some people have two distinct images: their *interview image* and their *employed image*. The person who was hired is the person who was at the interview. To change now would be unfair. Are you willing to put forth the same amount of effort you did for the interview day after day once you have the job?

If you want to make this relationship work, you will need to work at it and give it time. Hopefully, you will reinforce your employer's decision to hire you by being the kind of person your employer thought you were when you were hired.

Are you willing to put forth the same amount of effort you did for the interview day after day once you have the job?

Your Employer's Greatest Fears

A business executive who requested anonymity had this to say about today's young professionals: "The number one problem I've seen with employees fresh out of college is their inability to grasp the concepts of coming to work at the established time, coming to work every day, having backup plans when there are daycare issues, traffic problems, or weather problems. The idea of leaving for work a little early when the radio reports traffic backed up or weather problems just does not occur to them."

One of your employer's greatest fears is that he or she made a mistake in hiring you. A tremendous amount of time and money goes into the hiring and training process. Once you have been selected, other well-qualified prospects have been told they didn't make the cut. Your employer has made an enormous commitment to you by hiring you. If you end up working out really well, the person who hired you has succeeded and will be given credit for his or her hiring ability. If you don't work out, it will reflect poorly on the person who hired you.

Your employer believes in you and assumes you are everything you appeared to be in the interview. Be the kind of person your employer will value. Validate the decision this company made to hire you every single day. The way you present yourself is still important. So is arriving on time. Continue to watch what you say and do. In fact, everything you do from this day forward on the job will either enhance or detract from your reputation and advancement opportunities.

Taking on Your New Role: Your First Day

You will be meeting many new people on the first day of your job, and you will want to make a positive first impression with everyone you meet. Although first impressions are made rather quickly and based on initial judgments, the effects are long lasting. You need to think about your new role and the perception you want others to have of you.

One of your employer's greatest fears is that he or she made a mistake in hiring you.

The way you appear through your clothing choices, personal grooming habits, and the manner in which you carry yourself impacts the impression others will have of you. Evaluate and carefully plan for this new role you have assumed, and then do what's necessary to reinforce it every single day.

What kind of impression do you want to make your first day on the job? It will help if you make these decisions *before* you get to work. For example, let's assume that you want to appear friendly, confident, and professional. What do you think you will need to do to communicate friendliness, confidence, and professionalism? Let's take a look at each one individually.

Friendliness

In order to appear friendly, you have to be open and responsive to everyone you meet. You will need to be able to make conversation with others, be comfortable with yourself, make others feel comfortable around you, and appear interested in what others have to say.

Confidence

You don't necessarily have to feel confident to appear confident. If you carry yourself in a self-assured manner, others will assume you are self-assured. Start by standing tall, holding your head high, and looking directly at the people you meet. Doing this will help you project a sense of confidence, self-reliance, and comfort.

Professionalism

Consider the culture of the organization as you decide what to wear to work your first day. You are always better off being slightly overdressed than underdressed. (You will find more on clothing and appearance in Chapter 6.) Make sure you select a style that is flattering and appropriate for work. Pay attention to detail and make sure your clothing is clean, well pressed, and in good condition.

You are always better off being slightly overdressed than underdressed.

The following are additional tips for making a favorable impression the first day and reinforcing your new role:

- **Smile.** It may sound simplistic, but smiling is hardly simple. Many people take themselves and their work too seriously. People like to deal with people, not robots. A smile speaks volumes. A smile generally is received positively and then returned, communicating a positive message or "vibe" between the parties exchanging smiles.

- **Offer a handshake.** Once you get into the routine of coming to work each day it won't be necessary to shake hands with everyone you see. But on the first day, extend your hand to everyone you meet. This will help you establish yourself as a friendly and outgoing new employee. Make sure you offer a firm, strong handshake.

As you take on your new role as a professional, how will you look and act?

- **Make eye contact.** When you meet someone, look into their eyes long enough to remember their eye color. This usually amounts to about four to six seconds and is substantially longer than the one- to three-second glance we typically give someone upon being introduced. Prolonged eye contact helps you to connect with another individual and enables you to appear sincere when you say, "It's nice to meet you."

- **Remember names.** You will be meeting a number of people, and although it will be easier for others to remember your name because you are the one who is new, you will really make an impression if you remember the names of everyone you meet. One way to remember a name is through repetition. Use the name in conversation shortly after you hear it. You may want to associate the name with something or even write it down for reinforcement.

- **Be enthusiastic.** If you are enthused about your first day, it will be contagious to others. Show your enthusiasm through your smile, energy, positive attitude, and ability to listen.

- **Be on time.** Better yet, be early. Plan for any and all possible problems in advance. You don't have the experience yet to gauge the traffic, parking, and other factors involved with getting to work, so leave plenty of time for delays. You will be much more relaxed if you arrive early.

Playing the Part of a Professional

If you were the director of a play and had to advise the young lead actor how to "play the part" of a professional in a typical business environment, what advice would you give?

If the lead were male, would you suggest he wear a suit and tie? What about a female? Would you tell her to wear a mini skirt or a pantsuit? What details would be necessary to make the character believable?

How would you direct the actors as they try to "act" professional? What mannerisms would they need to capture?

As you take on your new role as a professional, how will you look and act?

Looking the Part

Whether consciously or unconsciously, each of us sends a message about who we are every time we interact with another person. Making sure you convey the appropriate message is important in establishing your credibility, no matter who you are or what you do. And since the clothing you wear is noticed before anything else, it's important to wear clothing that reflects your desired message.

Do you look and act like somebody who can do the job, not only the job you have now but the one you are striving for? You don't need to give up your individuality or compromise who you really are in order to look the part of a professional. There is plenty of room within the bounds of appropriateness for you to look and feel good about your appearance.

For your first day, select something that represents you well, keeping in mind you will be meeting many people for the first time. Clothing is the first thing noticed about a person, so look the part of a professional.

Acting the Part

You worked hard to get this job. You thought carefully about how you wanted to present yourself in the interview. Keep it up; whatever you did worked for you. You will want people to feel comfortable in your presence. Developing the skill of making others feel comfortable will pay off in the long run. People who are at ease (and put others at ease) in a variety of situations are viewed positively. Do you act like someone your co-workers, boss, and customers can work well with? Do you appear approachable and friendly?

Your actions are derived from what you say and, even more importantly, how you say things.

Your actions are derived from what you say and, even more importantly, how you say things. The way you carry yourself—your gestures and facial expressions—communicate much about you. Perhaps you've heard the expression "A picture is worth a thousand words." Your "picture" is how you appear to others and says far more about you than words could possibly say. What others see is what they perceive you to be. Act the part of a professional.

Being the Part

At first, some of what you do may feel forced or even phony, but if you continue to pursue these new behaviors, they become a part of who you are.

Do you look and act trustworthy? Are you the type of person others can depend upon? Most importantly, are you consistent? Can others depend on you to be this way every day? Can others count on you to do what you say you will do? In business, people tend to favor the expected over the unexpected. Consistency is the key. Be the kind of person you want to be and you will not only play the part of a professional but become one.

As an actor in a play, would you skip rehearsals and hope for your performance to come together opening night? You are about to take on your biggest new role yet. You want to give your best performance. No actor ever received a standing ovation without first planning and preparing for his or her role. How can you succeed without planning and preparing for your new role?

Plan who you want to be and where you want to go. On your first day on the job, look, act, and be the part of the professional you want to be. Your efforts will pay off. People will respond positively toward you and you will have a great experience your first day and, hopefully, every day thereafter.

On your first day on the job, look, act, and be the part of the professional you want to be.

Are You Ready for the World of Work?

Questions and Answers

True or False?

1.

One of your employer's greatest fears is that he or she has made a mistake by hiring you.

True. Remember, there are potentially hundreds of applicants applying for any one position. A tremendous amount of time, labor, and money goes into the process of reviewing resumes, interviewing candidates, and checking references. Therefore, making the decision to hire someone is not taken lightly. Hiring the wrong person can have huge ramifications, including the need to begin the process all over again. Once the decision to hire someone is made, a company wants nothing more than to move forward with this person. If you fail to work out, it is a costly mistake and the process will need to begin all over again. Don't enter into a job lightly. Make a serious commitment to be the same person you were during your interview.

2.

Introduce yourself to everyone in the office on your first day of work.

True. While you don't want to spend your entire day socializing or interrupting people who are diligently working, you will want to extend yourself to people you do not know. Although those who work there should extend themselves to you, don't wait for an introduction if they don't. Feel free to say hello and let people know who you are. It will make you, and others, more comfortable and help you to make a positive first impression.

3.

Once you get a job, you don't need to put forth as much energy as you did in the job interview.

False. The manner in which you conduct yourself during your interview should be a true example of who you will be day in and day out. If you act phony during the interview in order to get a job, you will not live up to the expectations of your employer. Try to go to work every day with the same kind of energy you had in the interview.

4.

Eye contact should be avoided when you first meet someone.

False. Avoiding eye contact could make you appear uncomfortable or insecure. When you meet someone and engage in conversation your focus needs to be on that person. Looking a person in the eyes is the most powerful way to connect with someone and communicates your interest and sincere intentions.

5.

Make sure you understand the expectations your employer has of you, and if unsure about something, ask for clarification.

True. Your employer will have many spoken and unspoken expectations about you. If you are unsure about anything, ask. Wondering about something or guessing will only create confusion. Asking questions shows that you desire to do well and that you are interested in fitting into your new environment. It also helps to eliminate misunderstandings that could lead to future problems.

6.

Repeating someone's name after an introduction will help you to remember it.

True. After you repeat the name, use it in your conversation. While you don't want to overuse the name, the more you use it, the more you reinforce it in your mind. Remembering someone's name shows that you care about and are interested in that person.

Chapter Summary

✓ Be a breath of fresh air in your workplace. Have a good attitude, be positive, and infect everyone with your enthusiasm.

✓ Be the kind of employee you said you would be during your interview, and don't let your guard down or become too comfortable in your position.

✓ Be proactive. Rise to the challenge of a bad situation. Take charge and solve workplace problems as quickly as they arise.

✓ Determine your commitment to your job. Stay committed and give yourself enough time to become acclimated to your new environment.

✓ Know your employer's expectations.

✓ Think of your employer as someone you are in a new relationship with. Work hard at making it a good relationship.

✓ If you have questions, problems, or concerns, talk to your boss or coworkers about them.

✓ Play the part of a professional: act, look, and be at your best every single day.

Chapter 5

Habits of Successful People

How Are Your Habits?

True or False?

1.

Successful people realize that it doesn't matter if people like you.

2.

It's okay to be a few minutes late for work as long as you get all of your work done in the time you are there.

3.

Conflict is bad and should be avoided whenever possible.

4.

If you are too complimentary to others, people may think you are insincere.

5.

A man should wait to see if a woman offers her hand for a handshake before offering his.

6.

It takes more than skill and knowledge to be successful.

Test yourself as you read through this chapter. The answers appear on pages 134-135.

Developing Good Habits

If you ever wondered what it takes to succeed, I can tell you that there are no secrets to success, and there isn't one particular thing that you can do that will make or break your career. Success seldom happens overnight, but if you are diligent, patient, and acquire good habits, you should be able to reach your goals. Some people excel by defying the odds, but most successful people have many qualities in common and possess many positive habits that make them successful.

There is a lot of information on the market about the importance of developing good habits. One of the best selling business books of all time is Stephen Covey's *Seven Habits of Highly Effective People* (Fireside, 1990). Businesses encourage employees to read books like Covey's and send them to seminars with the intent of helping them to embrace change and develop new habits in order to be more effective workers.

As a parent, I've tried to help my children develop many good habits: brushing their teeth, eating well, being on time, treating people respectfully, using good manners, showing appreciation, picking up after themselves, coming home on time or calling if they will be late, and so on. Some of these habits have been easier to instill than others.

Success seldom happens overnight, but if you are diligent, patient, and acquire good habits, you should be able to reach your goals.

I work hard at developing my own good habits and have had to break a few bad habits over the years. As a child, I had the habit of sucking my fingers. By the time I was four, my teeth protruded, my lips were puffy, and my fingers were swollen as a result. My parents did everything they could to get me to stop the sucking, but nothing worked.

My aunt finally came up with an idea. She enticed me by telling me that she would buy me a pearl ring once I stopped sucking my fingers. Even as a four-year-old I must have had an appreciation for jewelry because her offer motivated me to stop. Within a few weeks, my fingers and mouth were back to normal.

I began smoking cigarettes in high school, and when I married, I decided to quit. It wasn't easy, but I did it. It also wasn't easy when I had to give up my morning coffee for over a year while I experimented with ways to get rid of the headaches I was having, but I did.

Then there are habits I have wanted to acquire but never have. I've had the *desire* to make exercise a habit, read more for pleasure, and meditate every day. Although I exercise, I am not consistent in my efforts. I read for pleasure, but only on vacations, so that isn't a habit either. And I haven't taken the time to really understand meditation or learn how to incorporate it into my daily activities. I still intend to do these things, but haven't as of yet.

What Is a Habit?

So what exactly is a habit? *Funk and Wagnalls New International Dictionary of the English Language* defines a habit as:

"A tendency toward an action or condition, which by repetition, has become spontaneous."

You are likely to be presented with more opportunities throughout your career if you are able to develop good habits and take on some of the most common habits of successful people.

Jami, one of my closest friends, is addicted to exercise. I am in awe of her commitment to do some form of exercise every single day. I believe in taking care of myself and consider myself to be a healthy individual. I try to exercise often—and that may be my problem; *trying* isn't the same as *doing*. Exercising daily is challenging for me because my schedule changes daily. I've found it difficult to make exercise a habit—it's more of an effort.

Jami does some form of exercise every day. She will go out for a run in most any kind of weather and even exercises when she isn't feeling well. I've asked her how she motivates herself. Her reply: "Exercising for me is like brushing my teeth, it's a habit. If I miss a day, I don't feel right. I don't even have to think about doing it, it's just something I do automatically."

We all have habits—both good and bad. As you become part of a work environment, your habits will impact your success. You are likely to be presented with more opportunities throughout your career if you are able to develop good habits and take on some of the most common habits of successful people.

What are some of your good and bad habits? Are there habits you would like to eliminate and others you'd like to adapt? Think of as many of your habits as you can and list them in the space below. (If you don't own this copy of *How to Get a Job and Keep It,* write your responses on a sheet of paper.)

Good Habits	Bad Habits	Desired Habits
_____	_____	_____
_____	_____	_____
_____	_____	_____
_____	_____	_____
_____		

It Takes More Than Skills and Knowledge to Be Successful

A reporter from a South Carolina newspaper called me as I wrote this chapter. She was writing an article about dealing with difficult people in the workplace and wanted my input. She wanted to know how people should deal with a coworker who is habitually cranky or negative. One of the biggest sources of irritation for many people is learning to cope with a difficult person, which varies from someone who is simply annoying to someone who is bad-tempered.

It has been estimated that 85 percent of the reason a person lands a job, keeps a job, or moves ahead is due to their people skills, enthusiasm, and leadership ability. Only 15 percent of the reason a person lands a job, keeps a job, or moves ahead is because of his or her skills or knowledge.

Imagine you start out at a job the same time as someone else. Although you both have similar levels of knowledge and expertise, over the years one of you will achieve a greater level of success than the other. What do you think will determine who will be the one to excel?

Anyone can perform a task, and many people can do the same job. Once you have a skill or expertise, what will you do to make yourself stand out from your coworkers?

Once you have a skill or expertise, what will you do to make yourself stand out from your coworkers?

Sometimes there is so much focus on technical and product knowledge that the importance of people skills is overlooked. If you are pleasant to work with and make other people feel good about themselves, you will have an advantage in the workplace.

The Likability Factor

Typically, in addition to being effective in their jobs, successful people often are likable as well. Not only can these people perform the necessary tasks of a job, but they also have a way with people and a positive energy.

It will be difficult to be likable to others if you don't like yourself. If you are confident in yourself, you will radiate confidence. Although confidence often comes with age and experience, anyone can exude confidence. When you act confidently, you will feel and become confident.

The first time I had to speak publicly, I was terrified. I never expected to be a public speaker, yet as opportunities were presented, I knew I had to rise to the occasion. I would give myself pep talks before I began, and rather than stand before a group admitting my fear, I acted as if I were totally comfortable. As a result, I found it easier to actually feel comfortable. Sometimes an action has to come before the feeling in order to create a feeling.

If you want to develop good people skills and want people to like you, start by liking yourself.

If you are pleasant to work with and make other people feel good about themselves, you will have an advantage in the workplace.

How Likable Are You?

Answer yes or no to the following questions.

- Do you like people?
- Are you interested in what others have to say?
- Do you look on the bright side of things?
- Do you smile often?
- Do other people smile often at you?
- Are you a good listener?
- Do people confide in you?
- Are you a cheerful person?
- Do you compliment others easily?
- Are you happy with yourself?

If you answered yes to most of the questions, it is probable that you are very likeable.

Think about it.

Do you like people?

If you like people, you will approach all people positively and have a natural enthusiasm around others. As a result, people will enjoy being around you and, ultimately, like you, too.

Are you interested in what others have to say?

If you are sincerely interested in others, you will make people feel valued and cared about. Asking questions and taking an interest in others makes them feel important. If you make people feel valued, they will value you.

Do you look on the bright side of things?

If you are optimistic and tend to look on the bright side of things, people will enjoy being in your presence. There is plenty of gloom and doom in the world. Most people want to be hopeful and hear the positive spin on things.

Do you smile often?

A smile tells others you are happy and friendly. Some people never smile, and as a result, they come across as hostile or uninterested.

Do other people smile often at you?

If people smile at you, you probably smile a lot yourself and are viewed as approachable and friendly.

If you make people feel valued, they will value you.

Are you a good listener?

Do you listen when someone is talking rather than concentrate on what you want to say? Good listeners invite people to open up and show that they care about what is being said.

Do people confide in you?

When people confide in you, it is an indication they are comfortable talking to you and that they trust you. Consider yourself fortunate, someone confiding in you is a compliment.

Are you a cheerful person?

Given a choice, most people prefer to associate with cheerful people. Being cheerful is easy and uncomplicated and makes everything more enjoyable.

Do you compliment others easily?

Everyone can use a nice compliment—people crave appreciation. If you bring out the best in others, you bring out the best in yourself. Make others look good and you will look good in return.

Are you happy with yourself?

If you like yourself, people will notice and want to be around you. You will also find it easier to be supportive and complimentary of others if you are comfortable with who you are.

If You Like People, People Will Like You

Jeanne has worked for my family for years. She started out helping my mother with housework when I was a teenager and eventually began helping me once I was married and had a job. She has worked for my family for over 25 years. She has stayed with my children when I've been out of town and has been willing to do most anything to help me out.

Jeanne has worked for a number of other people over the years but hasn't stayed with all of them. One day, after I heard she quit working for someone I knew, I was concerned that she would be quitting me, too. Her response surprised me. She said, "Oh you don't have to worry about me leaving. I like you too much and I like working for you."

I felt so good as a result of her comment and realized that Jeanne wasn't just working for the money. She *liked* working for me. And you know what? I liked having her work for me, too. I still do. And I always thank her for her diligence, because I really do appreciate her.

Think of people you know who are likable. What similar characteristics do they possess? Almost anyone can become likable if they want to.

Frequently, people will come up to me after a seminar and ask me for feedback. They want me to assess how they are doing and how they come across. I rarely critique anyone without a specific objective but can tell anyone how to critique and evaluate him- or herself.

We all receive feedback from others every day, but sometimes we fail to notice. The feedback is evident by the way people respond to us. How do people respond to you?

Do You . . .

- Think people are difficult to get along with?
- Distrust people?
- Believe people are insincere?
- Consider people to be self-centered?
- Feel as though nothing good ever comes your way?

If you answered yes to any of the preceding questions, it is possible that you have negative expectations and, as a result, are likely to attract what you expect (negativity) rather than what you desire (good things).

A number of years ago, I worked with a woman who viewed everything negatively. She didn't trust anyone and believed that people were selfish and unreliable. She had issues with everyone and everything. She had trouble getting along with people at work, was frequently disappointed with her friends, and didn't get along with anyone in her family. I've never met a more discontented and dissatisfied person. I think she simply got in life what she expected.

On the other hand, there are people who believe that most people are good. Instead of expecting the worst, they expect the best and, as a result, attract good things and good people into their lives.

Get into the habit of recognizing the good in people and expecting good things to come your way.

Get into the habit of recognizing the good in people and expecting good things to come your way.

Embrace Enthusiasm

Think about a memorable concert or sporting event you've attended. What is the difference between attending these events live and watching them on television? Sitting in front of the television often provides a better view, but sitting in the stands surrounded by other fans often makes the event more exciting. A big part of that enjoyment comes from the energy and enthusiasm of the crowd.

Enthusiasm is contagious. When you reflect on the many teachers you've had over the years, the ones who stand out are those who loved teaching and were enthusiastic about their jobs.

In college I had a friend named Lisa. She was an only child, but she had many close friends, many whom she considered to be like a brother or sister. I used to tease her because, whenever I was with her, we always ran into people she knew and she always claimed each person was "like a brother or sister."

Lisa greeted everyone she met enthusiastically. Whenever I would call her, she would shriek with enthusiasm as she'd say, "Hi, Sue! How are you doing?" She was always excited to see or hear from anyone and, as a result, people loved being around her.

Over the years I evaluated what made Lisa so popular and well liked, and I attributed it to her enthusiasm. Although I considered myself a cheerful person, I wondered if I could increase my enthusiasm. If it worked so well for Lisa, imagine what some added enthusiasm could do for me professionally. I made an effort to make people feel important by acting excited when I would see them or hear from them. I even noticed a difference with my friends. A friend once told me that I always sounded tired and angry when I answered my phone, so I decided to answer with more enthusiasm. I am sure that my improved attitude encouraged my friends to call me more often.

Think about the people you enjoy associating with. There are people who light up a room when they enter it. You actually feel better just being around them. And then there are people who light up a room when they *leave* it. They are dull, boring, and depressing.

What does your presence generate? An increase in energy or a loss of it? Think about it.

Be Like Ruby

After a long day, I was ready to settle down in my hotel room, eat dinner, and get a good night sleep before my seminar the next day. Ordering and receiving room service is something I do frequently when I travel and is usually uneventful. But when Ruby, a room service worker, waltzed in and greeted me with her enthusiastic hello, welcoming me to Detroit, I was impressed.

She offered her hand for a handshake and began chatting with me as though we'd known each other for years. I had requested a pot of hot water to help me nurse the cold I was hanging on to, but it wasn't put on the order. Ruby was quick to assure me the water would be delivered. She went to the concierge to get it because it would be faster than going to the kitchen. When Ruby returned, she was so excited to be able to serve me in a beautiful silver pitcher. Concerned that I might burn myself, she instructed me to use the napkin when holding the handle.

The fact that Ruby was called back to my room because my order came undercooked didn't faze her. In fact, she was delighted to see me again and told me to be sure to ask for her the next night of my stay. It made me feel good to know that she cared so much.

The next night when I placed my order, I requested Ruby. When she came to deliver my meal, it was like greeting an old friend. "How is your cold today?" she inquired. We chatted about the day, and before she left I told her how impressed I was with her and that I wanted to send her a copy of my book, *How to Gain the Professional Edge.* Tears welled up in her eyes, and she told me that I had made her day. Then she gave me a hug.

Typically, hugging a customer would be taboo, but with Ruby it felt so real and so right. "I love people," she explained. "I get compliments all the time, and my boss told me to keep doing whatever I am doing because it's working. I love what I do and love people. I am blessed with the gift of loving people."

I mailed her my book and received a thank you note along with a picture she had taken of herself, smiling and holding the book. That picture sits on my desk. I meet many people in my travels, but Ruby is blessed with a gift, and she is some-one I will never forget.

Bless yourself with the gift of loving people. Develop the habit of being enthusiastic. The rewards will be abundant.

Value Yourself

Do you value yourself? Some people would say that Ruby's role as a server was insignificant—a low-level position in the hotel business. But think again. Without someone to serve food, how would a hotel take care of its guests? Every position is important, and Ruby had the sense to know that what she did mattered. In fact, she went beyond what was expected of her and reaped the benefits. She undoubtedly received bigger tips and positive feedback because of her exceptional attitude.

I frequently am asked how to deal with people (especially supervisors) who are rude, make unreasonable demands, fail to give promised raises or conduct reviews on time, and often degrade and demean their employees. It is no fun to work for someone who doesn't value you, but unless you value yourself and set boundaries, people will treat you however they want.

As I said earlier, many people get what they expect in life. What do you expect from other people? Do you expect to be treated respectfully? Do you expect people to honor their commitments? Are you willing to speak up when you feel you are treated unfairly?

Bless yourself with the gift of loving people. Develop the habit of being enthusiastic. The rewards will be abundant.

Learn to Stand Up for Yourself

My daughter Stephanie worked as a nanny for a family. They were going on a vacation and asked her to drive them to the airport. She agreed to take them even though it meant waking up at 3:30 in the morning in order to pick them up at 4:00 AM.

When Stephanie told me her plans, I was appalled. Not only was I concerned about her driving the 25 miles to and from the airport in the middle of the night, but anyone under the age of 18 is not supposed to be out driving after midnight or they could get a ticket. In addition, Stephanie had to work at her retail job the next day, and I knew she would be exhausted.

When I questioned her, Stephanie told me that she didn't really mind. More importantly, she didn't know how to decline and was fearful that the people she baby sat for would be mad at her.

"So what if they are mad at you?" I asked her. "You should be mad at them for asking you to get up in the middle of the night to drive them to the airport. They can call a cab."

I insisted she call and tell them she couldn't drive them, even giving her permission to blame it all on me. She was petrified of their reaction and begged me to let her drive them.

My husband and I talked about it and felt strongly that these people were taking advantage of our daughter. I ended up making the call to tell them that Stephanie was unable to take them to the airport. I told them that not only was it illegal for my daughter to be out driving after midnight but that we were uncomfortable with her being out in the middle of the night. The woman was most understanding and hadn't even been aware of the curfew.

The people you work with are part of a team. When you begin your new job, you will be the newest team member.

Why would Stephanie be more concerned about this woman's needs than her own? Why was she afraid to stand up for herself? Perhaps her age and her desire to please others played a role in her reticence. However, no matter what your age or circumstance, if you feel uncomfortable with a request someone makes, you need to speak up. If you are uncomfortable with the way someone treats you, address it. You need to be your own advocate. If you don't value yourself, why should anyone else? Placing value on yourself should be automatic. Make it a habit.

Be a Team Player

No matter what job you hold, your performance is important and you add value to an organization. Were you involved in sports in school? If so, you probably learned a lot about the importance of being a part of a team and how to be a team player. The people you work with are part of a team. When you begin your new job, you will be the newest team member.

Just as in sports, your workplace will have star players and those who appear to have it "better" than others. Don't expect too much too soon. Pay close attention to how things are done and try not to stray too far from the norm.

If you view yourself as part of a team, then you will realize that the work you do is significant and part of the whole. Don't isolate yourself. The job you do is essential but not the only important job to be done. Work with others and be willing to pitch in and help out even when the duty isn't in your job description. If you do, you will be viewed favorably by your team members.

Think in terms of being a part of a team—a good habit to have.

Giving and Receiving Compliments

Can you remember the last compliment you received? When was the last time you paid someone else a compliment? Are you free with praise for others? Some people hold back positive comments because they are afraid it will boost someone's ego too much or fear that complimenting others will somehow take away something from themselves.

Work with others and be willing to pitch in and help out even when the duty isn't in your job description.

Although some people become embarrassed when receiving a compliment, most people welcome a flattering remark. Your comfort level may reflect what you are used to hearing. If you grew up in an environment in which you received positive remarks about yourself, you may be comfortable giving and receiving compliments. If praise was withheld, you may find that you, too, hold back and aren't comfortable complimenting others.

People crave appreciation and will work harder to please you when they know their efforts will be appreciated. Successful managers know that praising an employee can be equally, if not more, important than financial rewards. Bob Nelson, a well-known speaker and author of the book, *1001 Ways to Reward Employees* (Workman Publishing, 1994), has made a business out of helping managers find ways to reward employees. Showing appreciation and complimenting others is not something that comes easily or naturally to many people.

Have you ever complimented someone only to have the person negate what you've said? I've noticed that many people do this. I teach a class on presentation skills, and because people are so uncomfortable speaking before a group, I've found that it is difficult for many people to accept any positive remarks about their presentations. In fact, I've had people challenge me when I've given positive feedback by trying to convince me that their presentation was terrible—refusing to accept my opinion.

If you are given a compliment, the best thing to do is to simply say thank you. Don't challenge someone's position or try to convince him or her that you don't deserve the compliment.

Look for the good in people and be free and sincere with your comments and compliments. People crave positive reinforcement. You lose nothing by giving positive feedback to others. In fact, you will gain. Every time I am able to make someone else look or feel good, I look and feel good, too.

In his book, *How to Win Friends and Influence People* (Pocket Books, 1994), Dale Carnegie says that giving honest, sincere appreciation is the key to dealing with people and that people will cherish your words and treasure them long after you have forgotten them.

When you pay someone a compliment, be specific. Rather than telling someone, "I liked your presentation," find something about the presentation you liked. For example say, "I liked it when you opened up and shared your personal experiences in your presentation. I feel as though I understand you and the importance of your message better now."

Try to avoid commenting too much on appearance as your intentions could be misunderstood. But do look for opportunities to bring out the best in others.

Get into the habit of complimenting and praising others.

Be on Time

Punctuality is one habit that many people find challenging. Rarely does someone plan on arriving late, but many people are consistently late for work, appointments, meetings, and other engagements. We've already discussed the importance of arriving on time and even a few minutes early for an interview, but being on time is equally as important once you have a job.

You may arrive late without hearing a comment from anyone, but, believe me, it is noticed. Of course there is the occasional tardiness that is acceptable and understandable due to bad weather, heavy traffic, emergencies, or illness. However, when you are habitually late, you begin to draw attention to yourself and your capability in other areas may be questioned. People may perceive you as negligent, disrespectful, disorganized, or incompetent.

If it is important to you to be on time, you will be on time. Therefore, when you are late for work or for an appointment, you are making the statement that you don't value your job or the time of the person you are scheduled to meet.

When you are habitually late, you begin to draw attention to yourself and your capability in other areas may be questioned.

Get into the habit of arriving a few minutes early. This way, if you do run into a problem, you will have the necessary extra time to work through it and still arrive on time.

If you say you will have something done by the end of the day, have it done by the end of the day. If you say you will call someone back by 5:00, call them back by 5:00. If you say you will do something, do it. If you miss too many deadlines or break too many promises, people will quickly learn that they can't depend on you.

People who are on time show that they are in control and have developed good habits.

Respect Others

Shortly after I began writing my syndicated column, I received a letter from a reader who claimed he was avoiding women at work because he was afraid of saying or doing something wrong. I wondered what he was so afraid of and told him that all he needed to do was to treat everyone respectfully and he wouldn't have anything to worry about. I was shocked at the enormous outcry from both women and men readers.

The women wrote to say, "Right on! This is what we want, to be treated equally and respectfully."

The men wrote that I was off base and that I had no idea what I was talking about. One man wrote that he was "walking on eggshells for fear of a woman slapping him with a lawsuit or harassment charge."

Many men and women are confused about their roles in the workplace. Test your understanding of gender issues by answering yes, no, or depends to the following questions:

- Should a woman wait for a man to offer his hand for a handshake?
- Should a woman expect a man to hold a door open for her and let her pass through first?
- Should a man wait for a woman to exit an elevator before getting off?
- Should a man or woman compliment someone on his or her appearance?
- Should a man help a woman on with her coat?

Following are some thoughts and insight on each of the questions.

Should a woman wait for a man to offer his hand for a handshake?

No. Men and women should always offer a handshake. It's a gesture of friendliness. There is no need to wait for a male to initiate it. And there is no need for a man to shake a woman's hand extra gently. A firm grasp is most effective.

Should a woman expect a man to hold a door open for her and let her pass through first?

No. If a man happens to be at the door and offers to hold it open, it is nicer than letting it slam in someone's face, but it is not a requirement. Nor must a man wait for all women to pass through before going through a door himself.

Should a man wait for a woman to exit an elevator before getting off?

Depends. If a man is at the front of the elevator and the woman at the back, it could be awkward if he waited for her to exit. Whoever is at the front of the elevator should get off first. If a man wishes to let a woman exit first, fine, but he shouldn't feel obligated to do so every time.

Should a man compliment a woman on her appearance?

Depends. A man can pay a woman a compliment as long as it is not about her looks or sexuality or is suggestive in any way. In other words, saying, "Wow, you look hot today" would be inappropriate, but saying, "That is a really nice suit you're wearing" could be okay. The danger in complimenting anyone about appearance is that it has the potential to be misunderstood. Your innocent comment could be taken the wrong way.

Should a man help a woman on with her coat?
Depends. Would this same man help another man on with his coat? If someone—male or female—is struggling, offer help, but don't assume that every woman wants or needs help putting on her coat.

Workplace Harassment

When I was in my early twenties, I worked six short months for a major corporation. Looking back, I realize I was quite naïve because I had no idea at the time that I was being sexually harassed.

I was one of three women among 20 male sales reps, and a number of the men would whistle and comment about my appearance daily. Their behavior made me feel uncomfortable, but I just assumed it was something all women had to tolerate. There was a lot of touching and hugging in the office, which I didn't really like, but I didn't know I had the power to stop or refuse it.

Today, employers are cognizant of the need for sensitivity training, and most companies have strict policies against discrimination and harassment. Women aren't the only ones who experience harassment. Anyone can experience discrimination and harassment, whether it is due to gender, race, age, or a physical disability. It is totally disrespectful and unacceptable in any situation to comment on personal traits or differences or to make anyone feel isolated or uncomfortable. There are laws to protect people from discrimination, and you need to know your rights and stand up for them. You need to know how to defend yourself without being too confrontational or

There are laws to protect people from discrimination, and you need to know your rights and stand up for them.

aggressive. If someone treats you in a manner that makes you uncomfortable, say something. Don't be afraid to hurt someone's feelings at the expense of hurting your own. (See Chapter 9 for more information on workplace discrimination and harassment.)

Get into the habit of treating everyone with courtesy and respect.

Manners Do Matter

The way you treat people reflects your values and feelings about them. Displaying good manners shows that you respect people. In the workplace, manners do matter. Common courtesies help put others at ease and show that you are knowledgeable and savvy.

Common courtesies help put others at ease and show that you are knowledgeable and savvy.

Little things make a major difference. Saying please when requesting something is less demanding than a command. Saying thank you when someone does something for you shows your appreciation.

Certain behaviors are considered crude and need to be avoided in the workplace. Chewing and snapping gum, burping and belching, and talking loudly or about inappropriate matters (Chapter 7 covers conversation in detail) need to be avoided.

Any action that has the potential to offend someone should be avoided, and includes telling offensive jokes, making inappropriate comments, touching, smoking, and swearing.

Your best insurance against offending someone is to be sensitive to others and to act with caution. If ever in doubt about something, ask your supervisor for guidance.

Common Workplace Courtesies

Saying please and thank you are common courtesies. Offering to help someone who is struggling with a task is a nice thing to do. In the dating world, men have been taught to help a woman with her coat, open doors, and to do a variety of polite and gentlemanly acts. In the business world, forget about the dating rules and stick with business behavior. Here are a few examples:

- If someone (male or female) needs help carrying something, offer to help.
- If someone (male or female) has full hands and can't open the door, grab the door and open it.
- If you are running to the coffee shop, offer to get something for someone else.
- If you use the last piece of paper in the copier or fax machine, refill the paper bin.
- If you finish the coffee in the coffee pot, make another pot of coffee.
- If someone is on the phone or talking with someone, don't interrupt.
- If you are about to begin a conversation with a coworker near others who are diligently working, go somewhere else so you won't disturb anyone.
- If you need a stapler, pencil, or paper clip, ask before you take it from someone's desk.
- If you borrow something from someone, return it.
- If you make a mess, clean it up.
- If you smoke, smoke in designated areas.

How you handle stress and the manner in which you deal with conflict will make a difference in the way you are perceived and impact your overall effectiveness on the job.

Be cognizant of the people around you. Treat others as you wish to be treated. It's common courtesy.

Solve and Resolve Problems

It is inevitable: you will be faced with challenges at different times throughout your career and life. How you handle stress and the manner in which you deal with conflict will make a difference in the way you are perceived and impact your overall effectiveness on the job.

Whether at work with managers, coworkers, or customers or at home with family and friends, we all deal with conflict at one time or another. Although many people will do almost anything to avoid conflict, it is impossible because conflict is an inevitable part of human relationships.

When the word *conflict* is mentioned, there often is a negative association attached to it. What are some of the thoughts that come to your mind when you think of conflict?

Many people associate conflict with negative emotions. Some common words associated with conflict are:

Anger	Frustration	Hostility
Problems	Power	Vulnerability
Disagreements	Fear	Controversy

The truth is that conflict isn't always negative. *Funk and Wagnalls New International Dictionary of the English Language* defines conflict as

> "A state or condition of opposition."

Disagreeing with someone isn't always bad. Many disagreements enable you to listen to a different perspective and, ultimately, gain new insight.

For example, my sister-in-law Maureen and I have engaged in stimulating discussions over the years. Although we have opposing viewpoints on a variety of topics from abortion to the death penalty, I have learned a lot and gained an appreciation for her views while not having to abandon my own.

In contrast, one time we were at a family gathering, and a number of us became involved in a conversation about abortion. The discussion became so heated that my mother-in-law insisted that we stop the discussion. That conversation wasn't as fun or stimulating as many others I've had. I realized it was because there was a lot of forceful preaching rather than discussing, listening, and respecting each person's point of view.

Conflict can be a vehicle, rather than a roadblock, to help you reach a new level of understanding. Many disputes can actually work *for,* rather than *against,* you. When you attempt to truly *resolve* a conflict rather than *resist* it, you have taken the first step toward using conflict constructively.

Do you watch television? Many television programs and talk shows thrive on conflict and controversy. Do you read suspense novels? Do you enjoy movies? Which type—dramas,

When you attempt to truly resolve a conflict rather than resist it, you have taken the first step toward using conflict constructively.

thrillers, action, or adventure? How about the evening news? Do you tune in or read a newspaper? Do you enjoy sporting events or watching people debate?

If you answered yes to any of these questions, then perhaps you do embrace conflict because all of these activities involve some type of conflict. Perhaps we are interested in viewing conflict because the conflict belongs to someone else. It is different when we are a part of the conflict.

I guarantee that you will experience conflict at some point in your professional and personal lives. Being prepared to deal with conflict will help you through trying times. The following tips will help you handle conflict:

- **Control your emotions.** Know your triggers and find a way to manage them. If you are easily frustrated or get mad over little things, work on calming yourself. When you feel yourself ready to blow up or lash out at someone, do what you can to get into the frame of mind to calmly deal with the conflict. Taking deep breaths or stepping away for a moment is sometimes all it takes.

- **Be open to others.** Be the type of person others are comfortable talking to and venting with, if necessary. If someone has a problem with you but cannot approach you, he or she is more likely to hold the anger in. Worse yet, he or she might gossip about you to other people. Encourage honesty and feedback from others and accept it graciously.

- **Be a good listener.** Studies have shown that most of us are poor listeners and that we retain only 25 percent of what we hear. This indicates that we miss 75 percent of what is communicated to us! Listen to what others are saying and, remember, you have two ears and one mouth. Use them proportionately.

- **Be empathetic.** Take the time to understand another person's point of view. Try to put yourself in their shoes. Even if you don't agree with someone, you can make an effort to respect and understand his or her point of view.

- **Be direct.** If you have a problem with someone, take it directly to that person. Avoid complaining, gossiping, or talking with others about a problem that doesn't involve them.

- **Take ownership.** Rather than pointing fingers and placing blame on others, ask yourself what you may have done to contribute to the situation.
When confronting someone, speak in terms of *I* rather than *you*. For example say "*I* feel as though we are all responsible for cleaning out the coffee pot" instead of "*You* never do anything around here. When was the last time *you* cleaned out the coffee pot?"

- **Address problems immediately.** If you are upset about something, address it. Don't hold in your feelings or you may build resentment, and one day you may explode!

- **Nurture relationships.** Take time to get to know the people you work with and to build solid relationships. If you are struggling with someone, make an effort to get to know more about him or her. Ask for a lunch date or take a break together. Strong relationships can withstand most conflict.

- **Respect others.** No matter what their title or rank, treat everyone equally and respectfully. When you respect others, you earn their respect in return.

- **Embrace change.** If you resist change, you are resisting the inevitable. View change as an opportunity to learn and grow. Work at becoming more easygoing and flexible.

Get into the habit of facing and dealing with all problems that you encounter.

How Are Your Habits?

Questions and Answers

True or False?

1.

Successful people realize that it doesn't matter if people like you.

False. There will be people who succeed who are not well liked. However, if people like you, your chances of success increase. If people like you, they will want to help you and everything you do will be easier. While you don't want to focus too much on what other people think, you do want to establish yourself as a decent person. Be kind, sincere, and the kind of person people like to be around.

2.

It's okay to be a few minutes late for work as long as you can get all of your work done in the time you are there.

False. There is a reason the workday begins and ends at a specific time. It provides structure to the day, and you are expected to be there on time. Arriving on time shows respect for your coworkers, yourself, and your job. Occasionally showing up late will be excused, but being habitually late will not. Make it a habit to be on time.

3.

Conflict is bad and should be avoided whenever possible.

False. Although conflict often is perceived negatively, you are always better off dealing with conflict than avoiding it. Ignoring conflict won't make a problem go away and can actually make it worse because the issue can fester and grow. People who stifle their feelings often create inner conflict. When handled properly, conflict can lead to new ideas and new ways of thinking.

4.

If you are too complimentary to others, people may think you are insincere.

False. People want to be acknowledged and crave appreciation. When you make someone look good you look good, too. You only risk being perceived as insincere if you are. Look for the good in people and be generous with kind words and appreciation. You will benefit as much as the people you are praising.

5.

A man should wait to see if a woman offers her hand for a handshake before offering his.

False. A handshake is a gesture of friendliness and should be offered to everyone you meet, male or female.

6.

It takes more than skill and knowledge to be successful.

True. Knowledge and skill are important, but if you lack enthusiasm, leadership, and people skills, you will limit your potential. To be effective you need to focus on more than just getting your job done. The more perceived value you bring to a company, the more valuable you will be to that company.

Chapter Summary

Remember:

✓ **It takes more than skill and knowledge to do a job well.** Eighty-five percent of the reason you will land a job, keep a job, or move ahead in a job will be based on your leadership skills, your ability to interact and get along with others, and your attitude.

✓ **Focus on your likability factor.** People who are friendly, positive, kind, and caring about others are more likable than those who are not. Anyone can be the kind of person others enjoy. Make an effort to reach out to others. If you like and care about other people, chances are people will like and care about you.

✓ **Embrace enthusiasm.** Be the type of person who lights up a room with your presence. Approach your work and everything you do with enthusiasm. You will have more fun and, ultimately, be more effective.

✓ **Value yourself.** Be your own advocate. No matter what job you do, your contribution is valuable. People can only take advantage of you if you allow them to.

✓ **Be a team player.** Learn to work with others and be willing to do more than is expected. When a team succeeds, everyone is a winner.

✓ **Learn to give and receive compliments.** Look for the good in others, and be the first to comment on a job well done. You will feel good and make others feel good as well. When you receive a compliment, accept it by saying thank you. Don't ever contradict someone's positive opinion of you.

✓ **Respect others.** How you treat others is a reflection of how you value them. Many of the issues relating to gender, diversity, and harassment at work could be eliminated if everyone lived with respect for others. Show your respect for others by treating everyone courteously and respectfully.

✓ **Learn to resolve conflict.** Don't shy away from or avoid conflict; you can't escape it. Treat problems as an opportunity to grow and learn. Go directly to the source of a conflict and find ways to work through the problems you encounter.

Chapter 6

Appearance Counts

How Image Savvy Are You?

True or False?

1.

The longer you work at a job, the less important your appearance becomes.

2.

All companies allow employees to dress casually.

3.

Select the latest fashions when purchasing clothes to wear to work.

4.

Any hairstyle is acceptable as long as your hair is clean.

5.

It is not necessary to wear socks or panty hose if the temperature outside is over 80 degrees.

6.

It is illegal for an employer to dictate what you can and cannot wear.

7.

If you want to look thinner, wear solid, dark colors.

8.

Wear dark colors when you want to exude more power and authority.

9.

Wearing a jacket with slacks or a skirt will help you look more professional.

10.

Leather clothing is not acceptable in all workplace environments.

11.

Caps, hats, and visors are acceptable in a casual workplace.

12.

Shoes should be the same color or darker than your skirt or pants.

Test yourself as you read through this chapter. The answers appear on pages 161-164.

Image Is Important

When I started my business, it was with the idea that I would help people improve their effectiveness in their jobs by becoming more professional in their appearance, behavior, and attitude. After being certified by the Professional Image Institute in Atlanta, I was ready to call on companies. I'll never forget the comment from the tenant who worked down the hall from my office. "You're into image consulting, aren't you?" he asked. I smiled as he continued, "So you tell men to keep their zippers up, and women to keep their blouses buttoned, right?" He thought he was being humorous and chuckled as he spoke, but I didn't see the humor. I wondered if others would take me seriously.

At first, it took a lot of courage for me to call companies and ask for an appointment, but once I had the opportunity to sit down and talk with a manager, human resource director, or president of a company, I discovered that many of them shared similar concerns about the image and behavior of their employees.

Everyone I talked with worried about certain employees who unknowingly sabotaged their careers because they didn't understand the relationship between personal appearance and opportunities for advancement. Addressing such sensitive and personal issues with an employee was something that many managers chose to avoid because it was such a difficult task. No one wants to be the one to tell someone that they have poor hygiene, bad breath, or outdated clothing. How do you tactfully inform someone you care about that they need to dress differently or get a new hairstyle?

Rarely is the topic of personal appearance discussed in employee reviews, yet I've heard countless stories from individuals who attribute a promotion or raise to the fact that they dressed better than they needed to and "looked" as though they were ready for advancement. I've also heard from managers who didn't promote someone because they didn't *look* as though they were ready to take on more responsibility.

Not only are there legal concerns about possible discrimination when approaching someone on such a personal level, but the subject is so sensitive that it's easier to avoid it

I've heard countless stories from individuals who attribute a promotion or raise to the fact that they dressed better than they needed to and "looked" as though they were ready for advancement.

or delegate it to someone else. So I was hired to do the dirty work that nobody else wanted to do, and my business began to flourish. Sometimes I would address a group of 30 people because one person in that group really needed to hear the message, but the company felt everyone could benefit as well.

You can gain something from this chapter whether you place importance on appearance or not. Fair or not, the way you look is important and, ultimately, may influence your future more than you realize.

What Does Your Appearance Say About You?

Image is a highly personal issue to most people. After all, what you wear and the way you look makes a statement about who you are and how you feel about yourself. Some people are very comfortable with their image and maintain the same look throughout their entire life. Others frequently experiment with new looks, changing clothing and hairstyles often, and never look the same for long periods of time.

Fair or not, the way you look is important and, ultimately, may influence your future more than you realize.

Most people agree that judging others on appearances alone is unfair. Some people simply have an advantage when it comes to appearance. But most people, even those who are conventionally good looking, would change something about their appearance if they could. One person might want to be taller, another longs to be shorter. One person feels too thin, the other too fat. Some people are blessed with great looks, which can be both an advantage and a disadvantage. If you are too good looking, people may resent you or view you as superficial. On the other hand, some people make negative snap judgments about people who are not conventionally attractive.

When it comes to success, what you do with what you have and how you present yourself is much more important than natural beauty. There are many people who excel in spite of their perceived shortcomings. Being comfortable with your-self is the key. When you are okay with who you are, you will radiate an inner and outer attractiveness. Take a moment to answer yes or no to the following questions:

- Does it take you more than a few minutes to decide what to wear each day?
- Do you frequently change outfits after getting dressed?
- Do you find shopping (when it comes to buying clothes) a chore?
- Do you often feel that you are either over- or underdressed for an occasion?
- Do you often apologize for your appearance?
- Do people say that you look younger than you are?
- Do you wear unusual colors or styles?
- Do most people dress better than you?
- Do you try hard to look trendy?
- Do you wear rings or earrings on or in places other than your fingers and ears?
- Do you have visible tattoos?
- Do you think you look *different* from everyone else?

If you answered yes to any of the questions, you have an opportunity to identify some areas you may be able to work on to improve your image. If you didn't answer yes to any of the questions, you may have less work to do but will still benefit by increasing your knowledge about the importance of your appearance and things you can do to enhance your image.

Does Image Matter?

Many people don't want to believe that image matters. People don't like the thought of judging a book by its cover or judging people on their looks, but the reality is that we all make decisions about people based on appearances. After all, initially it's the only information we have about someone.

Think about your favorite musicians. Many people have the ability to sing or play a musical instrument, but what is it that creates a superstar? It has a lot to do with image. Hundreds of thousands of dollars are spent creating and marketing just the right image for many superstars.

As a teen or young adult, you probably feel a lot of pressure to fit in—especially in the clothing that you wear. You might pay $50 or more for a particular brand of jeans that everyone is wearing when there are jeans mass marketed for under $20. Simple T-shirts can be purchased for less than $10, but the same T-shirt with the logo of a popular store or brand of clothing will sell for two to three times that amount, and people will spend more in order to display the logo.

The clothing we wear does more than serve the function of covering our bodies or keeping us warm. Clothing and appearance often define our status and how we feel about our environment and ourselves. This has been going on for centuries in all cultures around the world.

Some people purposely dress differently, adorning themselves in metal and chains and dying their hair unusual colors. This is done with one purpose in mind: to make a statement. These people certainly fit in with others who dress as they do, but not with the mainstream, and this is done intentionally.

Think about your group of friends. Do most of you tend to wear the same style of clothing? Perhaps many of you even wear your hair in a similar style. How do you feel around groups of people who dress differently than your group of friends? Do you view them as unusual?

The reality is that most of us feel more comfortable around people who look and act as we do. We tend to favor the expected over the unexpected, the usual over the unusual.

Imagine you are boarding a plane. You greet the flight attendant and look to the left into the cockpit. Two people are seated at the control panels. Both are dressed casually; one is wearing overalls and the other is in cut-off shorts and a Mickey Mouse T-shirt. One has sunglasses around his neck, the other a cap on backwards.

Assuming that these people are not passengers, who do you conclude is seated in the cockpit—the pilots or the mechanics? Most people would assume people dressed that way are the mechanics, but what if you discovered that these people were your pilots? Perhaps they had decided to dress casually on this day. Would you care?

Most people respond that that they would care and that it is important for a pilot to *look* like a pilot. But does it really matter what they wear? Let's look at a few more situations, and you decide if the clothing worn makes a difference.

Does It Matter . . .

- What is worn to a prom or a formal dance?
- What a bride and groom wear at their wedding?
- What you wear when you go swimming?
- What team members wear when playing a sport?
- What is worn to a costume party?
- What a priest, minister, or rabbi wears to conduct services?
- What a police officer wears when on duty?
- What an orchestra conductor wears when performing?
- What a nurse or doctor wears when seeing patients or performing surgery?
- What Olympic contestants wear when they compete?
- What a judge wears in the courtroom?

You will probably agree that in all of the above circumstances the clothing *does* matter.

Wearing the appropriate clothing to work can help you mentally prepare for the job. In addition, wearing the right clothing can help you feel a part of a team and enables others to identify you. Wearing what is *expected* enables us to identify people and their positions. The right clothing creates a sense of decorum.

Wearing the right clothing will help you project an image in which your clients, employer, and colleagues are comfortable.

Wearing the right clothing will help you project an image in which your clients, employer, and colleagues are comfortable. Because human nature is somewhat predictable, we know that most people feel comfortable with others who look and act as they do.

Why Did You Wear What You Wore Today?

What are you wearing right now? It probably depends upon where you are as you are reading this, but if I could see you, what do you think your clothing would tell me (or others) about you?

Are You Telling Me (or Others) . . .

I care about my appearance *or*
I don't care about my appearance?

I dress for the occasion *or*
I wear what I want?

I spend a lot of money on my clothes *or*
I don't spend a lot of money on my clothes?

I got dressed in a hurry *or*
I took my time getting dressed?

I pay attention to detail *or*
I don't pay attention to detail?

I care what other people think of me *or*
I don't care what other people think of me?

How quickly do you think I would I be able to determine these things about you? Do you realize it would only take me (or anyone else) a matter of seconds to determine how you feel about yourself and others, based solely on your appearance? It may not seem right, but we all make snap judgments about people based on their appearance.

When I speak about image in my seminars, I often ask audience members why they wore what they did that day.

Was It Because . . .
- It was the only item that was clean?
- It was the only item that fit?
- It was comfortable?
- It would keep you warm or cool?
- It was on top of the pile?
- It's Friday, and you always wear the same thing every Friday?

People often laugh as they realize they sometimes wear things for the wrong reasons or for no reason at all. Wearing something because it fits your mood may do nothing to help you connect with other people or enable you to achieve your objectives. Considering the fact that your appearance communicates loudly about who you are, you should really think about what you wear every day.

What Does Your Clothing Say About You?
The way you present yourself makes a statement about how you feel about yourself. Your clothing is the first thing people notice about you and communicates many things. What you

wear and your attention to detail *will* be noticed whether you want it to or not.

Your Clothing Can Communicate:
- Your sense of style.
- Your level of success.
- Your social rank.
- Your feelings about yourself.
- Your feelings about your job.
- Your level of sophistication.
- Your financial status.

Think about a day when you weren't feeling well. Perhaps it was a day when you wished you could stay home in bed but couldn't. Would you put on a favorite outfit or opt for something that more closely matched your feelings?

When we feel lousy, most of us prefer to look lousy, too. In fact, on a lousy day, we may actually look for something lousy to wear rather than putting on something that we typically feel good in.

Imagine that you feel lousy but put on one of your favorite outfits. Do you think it would affect the way you feel? Even if you don't feel well but you fix your hair and dress up, you may find that you actually feel better.

Something happens when we go through the process of getting ready for work. Whether applying make up, styling your hair, or putting on a uniform, each step helps you to physically and mentally prepare for your role at work. When you look as though you took the time to prepare yourself for your role, people notice. You are telling people that you take yourself and your job seriously.

When you look as though you took the time to prepare yourself for your role, people notice. You are telling people that you take yourself and your job seriously

Fads Come and Go, But Classics Are Forever

Having three teenaged daughters, I am well aware of the importance many teens place on fads. I cannot tell you how often I have heard one of my daughters tell me that she *has* to have a certain piece of clothing or pair of shoes.

When it comes to dressing for work, unless you are in the fashion industry, you don't have to worry about wearing the latest fad. You will want to look up to date, but understated is definitely better than overstated.

When you invest in classic clothing (clothing that rarely goes out of style), you don't have to worry about buying the latest fads, and you will be able to wear your clothes season after season.

As you begin to put together your work wardrobe, be patient. It can take years until you feel you have a solid wardrobe. When you make a purchase, select basic styles in jackets, slacks, shirts, and skirts. Neutral, solid colors enable you to mix and match a garment with other pieces.

Think about it. A black pair of slacks can be worn a number of days in a week and paired with different jackets, shirts, or tops, and no one would know you were wearing the same slacks. However, if you wear a plaid jacket, not only will you have fewer options as to what to put with it, but because it is unique, it will be remembered.

Casual Can be Complicated

Dressing casually in the workplace is a privilege, although many people consider it to be the norm. Years ago, it would have been difficult to imagine going to work dressed in jeans, but today many people do. However, jeans are not considered typical business attire.

Although some people claim that dressing casually increases efficiency, others feel it decreases the decorum in an office. Some people believe that casual dress is here to stay, while others say it is on its way out.

Several years ago, I was interviewed for an article on business casual. You may not realize it, but dressing casually was a very big change to hit the American workplace not too long ago. The interviewer asked me if I thought that we would ever go back to more formal dress codes. Most people assume that once a company goes casual that there is no turning back. I replied that although I believed casual dress was here to stay, I could foresee a backlash at some point in the future. If people take dressing casually for granted and become too careless in their appearance, a company may be forced to implement stricter guidelines. I've seen it happen already.

When casual first crept into the workplace, men simply removed their ties and women were able to wear slacks instead of skirts. By today's standards, casual dress was fairly formal in the beginning. But as time has elapsed, people have become more and more casual, many to the point of looking sloppy. As a result, companies have made dress provisions in their guidelines.

Some companies have decided that jeans are no longer acceptable, while other companies have gone back to formal dress every day except Friday. Still other companies have retained a casual dress code on most days but instituted Formal Fridays and Dress Up Days to regularly encourage a more formal atmosphere.

Employees may enjoy dressing casually, but not all customers appreciate the relaxed attire. After all, sometimes it is difficult to distinguish an employee in an office from the delivery person, and in a retail establishment, this can be a problem if it is difficult to identify someone to help you.

I was called in to help create and present clothing guidelines to 400 employees of a bank after a customer closed her account and took her business elsewhere. The reason: she didn't like discussing her financial matters with a person who looked as though he was ready to clean his garage.

The customer was so offended by the appearance of the bank teller that she closed her account. She actually did the bank a favor by telling it the real reason she left, and it was able to do something about it.

What you wear often is dictated by customer expectations and the industry you work in. The more conservative the industry, the more conservatively you'll need to dress. Young and creative companies have much more latitude when it comes to image and clothing.

If you can't stand the thought of wearing a suit but you are in a career in a conservative industry, you need to realize that your industry, not your preference, dictates what you should

What you wear often is dictated by customer expectations and the industry you work in. The more conservative the industry, the more conservatively you'll need to dress.

wear. In traditional and conservative industries, conventional attire is the norm.

It will be important for you to find out if there is a dress code in your workplace and if there are guidelines in place. Many companies assume that employees know and understand what is acceptable and what is not, which may lead to some confusion about what is expected. Guidelines are helpful because they leave little to personal interpretation.

When you think of casual dress, what comes to mind? Many people think of shorts, T-shirts, sweatpants, and jeans. Many people equate casual dress with casual activities, such as relaxing, running errands, exercising, and cleaning. However, a casual work environment is, and should be, different. Unless you are a laborer or work in manufacturing, T-shirts and jeans are prohibited in most professional environments.

Business Casual Taboos

The following styles are never recommended, even in a very casual environment:

• **Sweats.** Sweatpants and sweatshirts are much too casual to wear in the workplace.

• **T-shirts with slogans or graphics.** You may think the saying you're wearing is hysterical, but it could be offensive to someone else. Unless you are wearing a T-shirt with the company logo, don't promote any other business or manner of thinking.

• **Oversized clothing.** I realize that baggy pants riding below the waist are fashionable in high school and on campus, but they aren't appropriate for the workplace. Loose-fitting clothing looks sloppy.

• **Undersized clothing.** Call it *undersized* or simply *too tight,* but don't pretend your clothes fit when they don't. The tighter the garment, the more you risk appearing suggestive or, worse yet, unsightly.

• **Spandex.** Tight clothing draws attention to the body. This can be distracting to others and is not recommended in the workplace. Save the spandex for after hours.

• **Shorts.** Shorts are too casual for most business environments. If your company allows shorts, wear them, but wear them a bit longer than you would in a casual setting: no short-er than a few inches above your knees.

• **Mini skirts.** Skirts are fine as long as they aren't too short. Anything several inches above the knee is too short.

• **Sleeveless tops.** Even when it is warm outside, it isn't profes-sional to expose too much skin. On women, sleeveless tops tend to reveal undergarments, which are supposed to be out of view. Many halter and tank tops are cut so low that cleavage is visible, which is unthinkable in a business environment.

• **Swimwear.** Forget about wearing bathing suits, cover-ups, or anything that resembles something you would wear on a hot, sunny day at the beach.

• **Loungewear.** Some loungewear resembles pajamas, and obvi-ously pajamas are for sleeping, not for working. Loungewear enables you to lounge. Workplace attire enables you to work.

• **Athletic shoes.** Beware: people will notice your shoes. Do not wear dirty, worn out sneakers or any footwear that you would wear to exercise.

• **Sandals.** Unless you are given permission to wear sandals or go without socks, you will need to wear socks and closed shoes at work. Sandals cover a wide range of styles, and while some may be acceptable, many are too casual and lack sufficient cov-erage for the workplace. If you are allowed to go without socks, make sure your feet are in top condition.

• **Vintage clothing.** Styles come and go; wearing something from a different era will make you look as though you are stuck in that era.

• **Headgear.** You couldn't wear headgear in school, and you can't wear it in the workplace either. Hats, caps, and visors are not to be worn in the workplace unless they are part of a uniform.

Important Factors to Consider

You will make many decisions that impact your career. One decision that you will make every day is what you wear. This decision will affect the way you feel and create a certain feeling among others. In order to present yourself in the best possible manner, there are a number of factors you must consider when deciding what to wear.

Your Personal Style

What works for someone else may not work for you. If you are uncomfortable dressing causally, don't. You are always better off dressing up a bit than looking too casual. It may take some time to develop your own sense of style but never force yourself to wear a style or color that you are uncomfortable wearing unless it is required.

Your Customers

What do your customers expect of you? If you needed to hire an attorney, what would you expect the attorney to look like? If you were working with an accountant, what would your expectations be? What about an advertising executive? Dress in a manner that shows respect for yourself, your company, and your customers.

Your Employer

Your employer expects you to represent the company professionally and to be consistent in your appearance. If you have concerns or questions about what to wear, ask your supervisor.

Your Industry

Take into your consideration the nature of your industry. If you work for a high tech or graphic design firm, the dress expectations will be different than if you work in an established, traditional industry, such as accounting or banking. Each industry has its own image standards; know the standards of your industry.

Dress in a manner that shows respect for yourself, your company, and your customers.

Your Position

Your position within a company and the functions of your job will influence what you wear. If your job requires you to be physically active (bending, moving, etc.), you will need to dress accordingly. If you have a low-level position, don't assume your appearance doesn't matter. Sometimes it helps to dress for the position you *want* to have to help appear ready for that position.

The Climate

Although most offices are climate controlled, weather does play a role in what you will wear. The biggest challenge comes in very hot weather. People want to eliminate as much clothing as they can in order to be comfortable, but in business, removing too much is not advised.

What You Can Wear: Business and Casual Options

Hopefully, your company will provide you with guidelines for business and casual dress, but even if they do, some guidelines may be vague. Managers don't want to become the fashion police, and hope you will use good judgment in your clothing selection.

Simple, tailored clothing works best in business. The following clothing choices for men and women are listed in order from most professional to most casual.

Women:
Skirted suit
Pantsuit
Skirt with jacket
Dress with jacket
Dress
Skirt and vest
Skirt and blouse
Slacks with jacket
Slacks with vest
Slacks with blouse or sweater
Casual pants with casual shirt
*Jean skirt with vest, blouse, or sweater
*Jeans with jacket
*Leggings with long sweater
*Jeans with sweater or shirt
*Walking shorts with shirt (shorts should be no more than a
    few inches above the knee)

Each industry has its own image standards; know the standards of your industry.

*Note: Jeans, shorts, and leggings as casual options are not acceptable in all workplaces. It is important that you find out what your company's policy is on these items before you chance wearing them to work.

Men:
Suit
Slacks with sport coat or blazer
Slacks, dress shirt (no tie), and jacket
Slacks with sweater and jacket
Slacks with dress shirt and tie
Slacks with sweater
Casual slacks with casual shirt and jacket
Casual slacks with casual shirt and tie
Casual slacks with polo shirt
*Jeans with shirt and jacket
*Jeans with shirt or sweater
*Walking shorts (no more than a few inches above the
    knee) with shirt

*Note: Jeans and shorts as casual options are not acceptable in all workplaces. It is important that you find out what your company's policy is on these items before you chance wearing them to work.

Whether you work in a casual environment or not, you always have the option of dressing better than required. Dressing better than you need to can actually make you appear as though you are taking your job more seriously.

Dressing better than you need to can actually make you appear as though you are taking your job more seriously.

Craig Kaminer, president of Influence, LLC, a strategic marketing, communications, and Internet development agency, recalls his first job as the director of public relations at the Jan Stuart Corporation, a manufacturer and marketer of upscale fragrance and skin care products. The office environment was very casual. A warehouse took up most of the space in the building; there were just 10 executive offices. Craig's office was located immediately next to the owner, Jan Stuart.

When he started the job, fresh out of college, Craig wanted to fit into the executive ranks of this well-known Seventh Avenue company. And while he was told he could dress casually whenever he wanted, he soon discovered that dressing down would not help him move up in the company.

On the days he dressed casually, Craig noticed he was asked to do things outside of his job description. Jan would ask him to get him coffee, pick up a newspaper, or run an errand. Yet when Craig wore a suit and tie, he noticed that he was never asked to do these odd jobs. He soon realized that running errands wasn't asked of an executive with an important position and that when he looked like an executive, he was treated like one.

Upon this realization, Craig stopped dressing casually, and within a short amount of time, he was promoted. Craig has spent most of his career making sure he plays the part of the person he wants to be. Even now, as president of his own company, he believes his image plays a big role in his success.

Additional Wardrobe Tips: Putting Your Look Together

Color

Did you know that if someone is wearing a color you do not like that you might not trust that person? Color influences us and affects our moods and emotions. Each of us responds differently to colors.

Imagine you've just won a brand new car, and you get to pick the color. What color would you choose? Would it matter? Maybe you would be so happy to have the car that it wouldn't matter, but you probably have a preference if given a choice. Color is an important factor when selecting the car you drive and it is just as important when selecting your clothes.

Neutral colors (black, navy, gray, tan, brown) are considered basic colors and enable you to mix and match with other clothing in your wardrobe. Red and blue are staple colors as well. People may notice and remember the bright orange and yellow striped slacks you wore, but rarely will someone think twice about a black or other neutral-colored garment.

Build your wardrobe by purchasing suits, slacks, skirts, and jackets in neutral colors and accenting with other colors through blouses, shirts, scarves, and ties. In general, darker colors project confidence and strength. Lighter colors, which are softer to the eye, enable you to appear less threatening and more approachable.

Fabric

Pay attention to the fabric of a garment because it will determine how well something will wear. If the fabric looks wrinkled on the hanger, it will probably look wrinkled on you. You can test a garment's fabric by the wrinkle test. Take a handful of the fabric in your hand and squeeze it tightly, then let it go. Is the fabric still wrinkled or did it smooth out?

The way it looks after the wrinkle test is the way it will look on you when you wear it. You don't want to wear wrinkled clothing, so select fabrics that wear well. Wools, wool blends, and some synthetic fabrics wear beautifully.

Fit

One of the most important aspects of looking good is achieved by wearing clothing that fits properly. An expensive garment will look cheap if it doesn't fit properly.

You want to make sure that your pants are long enough (pants should cover the top of your heel and break at the instep) and that your sleeves hit the wrist bone. Linings should never show, and seams and buttons should lay flat, with no pulling. You want to be able to move, sit, and stand comfortably. A good tailor can do wonders for you and generally can fix most problems.

When shopping and buying clothes for work, keep in mind that you get what you pay for.

Shopping

When shopping and buying clothes for work, keep in mind that you get what you pay for. If you buy inexpensive clothing in lightweight fabrics, you may find that they don't hold up well. This doesn't mean you need to spend lots of money on your clothes.

Some of the finer department stores offer personal shopping services at no charge. This is a great way to have someone shop for you and provide you with advice as you build your work wardrobe.

In addition, discount retailers offer the latest fashions at discounted prices and can be a great place to find good quality clothing.

Care of Clothing

Always wear clean, well-pressed clothing. You don't want to show up for work in something that looks like you slept in it. Taking the time to press your clothing is important. Some garments require dry cleaning, so read labels before cleaning. Certain fabrics tend to fade from the washing and drying process. Do what you can to keep your clothing from fading and don't wear anything that looks old or shabby.

Use a lint brush to keep your darker clothing from collecting animal hair and lint. If you have clothing that is frayed or filled with little balls of fabric, it may not be in good enough condition to wear to work. Wear clothing that is in top condition and do whatever you can to keep it that way.

Adorning Yourself

Personal adornment has become increasingly popular in our society. Many people like to uniquely distinguish themselves with body art. Although more accepted now than in the past, some body art can be a distraction in the workplace. The following sections discuss some of the most popular forms of body art.

Piercings

Pierced ears have always been fairly standard for women. However, wearing three or more earrings in one ear is not considered the norm.

If you are a male with pierced ears, you may want to think twice before showing up for work with earrings. As with everything, it will depend upon the industry you are working in.

Pierced noses, lips, and eyebrows are viewed differently and often more negatively than pierced ears. If this is a concern for you, consider taking the rings out for work.

If you are a photographer or artist or work in the fashion industry, the jewelry you wear won't matter as much as if you work in insurance, finance, or other conservative industries. Look around and notice what others are doing and wearing.

Tattoos

If you have visible tattoos, you may need to find ways to cover them. Tattoos can be distracting, offensive, or unattractive to others. One company I worked with had a strict policy about tattoos; anyone with visible tattoos had to cover them up. This meant that women with tattoos on their legs either had to wear pants or opaque tights so that they would not show and men with tattoos on their arms were prohibited from wearing short sleeves.

You may not be able to do anything about tattoos you already have, but when making decisions about getting additional tattoos, consider placing them in inconspicuous areas.

Jewelry

When it comes to wearing jewelry, keep it simple. Any type of noisy or gaudy jewelry is not recommended. Avoid extremely large earrings and keep the number of rings and bracelets to a minimum. One popular look is to wear many bracelets on one hand. This is fine as long as they don't get in the way of your doing work or make noise every time you move your arm.

Other Components of Your Appearance

Shoes

You may think your shoes won't be noticed, but they will. Wear comfortable shoes, but avoid wearing sneakers or shoes that are in poor condition. Avoid heels higher than three inches for ease in walking and standing. Keep your shoes in great condition by regularly cleaning and polishing them. You want to be dressed well from head to toe. The shoes you wear can pull together or tear apart a professional look.

Hair

For many people, a change in hairstyle takes place as they make the transition from student to professional. A study directed by Yale University researcher Marianne LaFrance (and commissioned by Procter & Gamble), found that people make a variety of judgments about new acquaintances based on their hairstyles. The study reported that different hairstyles were found to create the following impressions:

- **Women with short hair:** perceived as confident and out-going, but the least sexy.
- **Women with long, straight, blonde hair:** perceived as sexy, affluent, but narrow-minded.
- **Women with medium-length, casually styled, dark hair:** perceived as good natured and intelligent.
- **Men with short hairstyles:** perceived as sexy, confident, but self-centered.
- **Men with medium-length hair and a part on the side:** perceived as intelligent, affluent, but narrow-minded.
- **Men with long hair:** perceived as good-natured, but also viewed as careless and unpleasant.

LaFrance also studied the effect of bad hair days on self-esteem. She found that when having a bad hair day people felt less capable, less smart, and less sociable.

While there isn't one particular look to recommend, there are some hairstyles that are more flattering and more mature looking than others. Long, straight hair is very common among college and high school females. If you wear your hair that way be aware of the message it sends, which is a youthful one. You might consider putting it up. Men's hair length generally should not go below the nape of the neck and should be cut in an up-to-date style. The most important aspect of hair is that it be clean, styled, and in good condition.

Change Is Good

Don't be afraid to change your hairstyle. A good stylist should be able to offer suggestions. Look for a stylist who will ask questions about your lifestyle and your preferences before cutting your hair. As with many other elements of your appearance, consider your industry and your position when deciding on the best hairstyle for you.

Hair Color

Many people color or highlight their hair. This is fine as long as you maintain the color. Coloring your hair in an unusual color is not recommended, nor is having the roots of your hair a different color from the rest of your hair. Both are very unflattering looks and unprofessional. Visit your stylist on a regular basis, touch up your color, and take care of your hair.

Maintain healthy hair by using quality hair products and getting regular haircuts. Select a style that is easy to maintain so that you will be able to have great looking hair every day without spending too much time on it.

Facial Hair

For men in business, a closely shaved face has always been the most universally accepted look. Although facial hair used to be considered a deterrent in business, it isn't a problem for most men today.

Many men feel that facial hair enhances their features. Men with a baby face often feel they are at disadvantage. Growing a mustache or beard is one way to appear older. Men with receding hairlines often grow facial hair to compensate for their hair loss on their head.

Pay attention to people in high-level positions. You will probably notice that the majority are clean-shaven. If you watch the television news, you rarely see male anchors with facial hair. Perhaps it is because facial hair can be distracting and sometimes is viewed negatively.

Full beards are viewed less favorably than mustaches, partly because beards cover the face, making it difficult to see what lies beneath. Being able to view the expression on someone's face is important. If people can't "read" you, they may not understand you.

Many men are very attached to their facial hair. Ask a man with a mustache how long he has had it, and you will probably learn it has been a part of his "look" for years. It's good to vary your appearance over the years. If you stick with one look your entire life, you risk looking as though you are trapped in a time warp.

If you choose to wear facial hair, you will need to keep it neatly trimmed: don't let it grow too long or shaggy. Be especially careful when you eat, and make sure you don't have food in your mustache or beard. While facial hair is acceptable, hair in other places is often viewed negatively. Pay attention to unwanted and unruly hair growth in your nose, ears, and eyebrows. If you have stray hairs, cut them, as they can be distracting.

Obviously, women don't choose to grow mustaches or beards, but some women do experience hair growth on their face and chest. Many women choose to remove the unwanted hair, but some do not. While light facial hair is common and not a problem for most women, dark hair is much more visible and is often considered unattractive. There are many permanent and temporary methods of hair removal. If facial hair is a problem for you, consider having it removed.

Hands

Did you know that people notice your hands? You use them when you shake hands with someone, when exchanging business cards, and when writing, typing, speaking, and eating. Your hands are especially visible to other people and are an important part of your overall image.

Pay attention to your hands. Dry, chapped hands, ragged or bitten nails, hangnails, and dirty fingernails will be noticed and may send a negative message to others. If you bite your nails, try to break the habit. Not only will it be distracting if you bite them in front of others, but people who bite their nails may be considered nervous or anxious.

Clean and well-manicured hands show that you pay attention to detail. Long, clawlike, and decorated nails are not the norm in the workplace. If you wear acrylic nails, don't wear them too long. Fingernail polish is fine, but stick to traditional colors and avoid purples, black, and fluorescent colors.

When it comes to your image, little things make a big difference. Pay attention to detail, and present yourself in the best possible manner.

Pay Attention to Detail

When it comes to your image, little things make a big difference. Pay attention to detail and present yourself in the best possible manner.

Be Sure Your . . .

- Clothing is clean and free of spots or stains.
- Clothing fits properly.
- Clothing is well pressed.
- Clothing is in good condition: no holes, rips, or tears.
- Clothing is free of lint and animal hair.
- Shoes are polished and in good condition.
- Hands are clean and well groomed.
- Hair is clean, styled, and up to date.
- Roots are the same color as the rest of your hair.
- Undergarments aren't showing.
- Make up is blended.

Grooming and Hygiene

I can't think of a topic more sensitive than that of personal hygiene. I want to assume that most people know and understand the importance of bathing daily and wearing fresh clothing and undergarments, but I've learned that not everyone does. You will likely, at some time or another, encounter someone with poor hygiene. Although it may be none of your business, it becomes your business when you are distracted or offended by someone else's hygiene.

Most people with poor hygiene have no idea how offensive they are to others. One reason is because we become accustomed to our own scent within about 15 minutes. We may be totally unaware of the stench we are carrying around.

Many people try hard to smell good and overcompensate by wearing too much perfume or cologne. Because many people are sensitive or allergic to perfume, you need to be cautious about what and how much you spray on yourself. For people who are allergic, perfume can induce sneezing, headaches, or an asthmatic reaction. It is best to avoid wearing fragrance at all, but if you must, wear fragrance sparingly.

How Image Savvy Are You?

Questions and Answers

True or False?

1.

The longer you work at a job, the less important your appearance becomes.

False. Your appearance will always be important. From the first interview until your last day on the job, the way you look impacts others and makes a statement about how you feel about yourself, your coworkers, and customers.

Many people mistakenly believe that once they have a job, it's safe to let their guard down. Assuming there is no need to impress anyone, they become remiss in their dress and, ultimately, their attitude.

2.

All companies allow employees to dress casually.

False. Casual dress is prevalent, and most companies allow employees to dress casually at least one day a week, but not all companies do. Therefore, if the company you work for does permit casual attire, do not take it for granted and view it as a perk. Due to the careless manner in which many people dress in a casual environment, companies have had to rethink their policies and some have reversed their casual dress codes, returning to a more structured dress code. Don't assume companies will always be casual. Trends come and go and it is possible that casual dress could someday become a thing of the past.

3.

Select the latest fashions when purchasing clothes to wear to work.

False. Unless you are in the fashion industry, some of the latest fashions may be too trendy or unprofessional for the workplace. What is acceptable in the workplace is a far cry from what you see in fashion magazines or on MTV. Invest in classic clothing that won't go out of style. Solid, dark colored skirts, slacks, and jackets are basic pieces that can be worn with a variety of tops and accessories.

4.

Any hairstyle is acceptable as long as your hair is clean.

False. Can you think of anything you wear that you have worn for 10 or 15 years? Styles change over time, and your hair is no exception. If you are wearing your hair in the same style you have for years, or even as recently as high school or college, it may be time for a change. If you are wearing professional clothing and your hair isn't in sync with your style, you ruin your efforts. Your hair should be clean, healthy, and styled for work every single day.

5.

It is not necessary to wear socks or panty hose if the temperature outside is over 80 degrees.

False. Unless your workplace tells you socks or panty hose are not required, wear them. Sometimes it is a health issue, and other times, a practical issue.

Not everyone takes care of their feet, and not everyone wants to see the feet of their coworkers. In a professional work environment, socks and hose are recommended, even when it is hot out. Lucky for all of us, most workplaces are air-conditioned.

6.

It is illegal for an employer to dictate what you can and cannot wear.

False. An employer has the right to have a dress policy and to enforce it as long as it doesn't discriminate against anyone. Think about all of the environments in which uniforms are required and in which an employer has the right to enforce proper dress. Even if you don't wear a uniform, there are standards in many workplaces. Ask if your company has a policy and become familiar with it.

7.

If you want to look thinner, wear solid, dark colors.

True. Solid, dark colors create a slimming look. However, you can add color to your wardrobe with blouses, ties, and accessories. And you don't have to wear one solid color. Because our eyes are drawn to lighter colors, wear darker colors in areas you want to appear slimmer.

8.

Wear dark colors when you want to exude more power and authority.

True. Darker colors project strength and help you come across with more authority. Think about the way politicians and attorneys dress, often in a dark suit, which may help them to look influential. You can use color to help you achieve your objective. If you look very young, wearing darker colors can help you appear more mature. Lighter colors, on the other hand, can make you appear more open and approachable.

9.

Wearing a jacket or blazer with slacks or a skirt will help you look more professional.

True. A jacket adds a touch of professionalism and a sense of completion to most any outfit. A simple blazer or jacket in a solid, dark color is something you will be able to wear with many different looks, and will be a valuable addition to your wardrobe.

10.

Leather clothing is not acceptable in all workplace environments.

True. Leather skirts, slacks, and jackets are readily available, but these garments are different than the same garment made out of wool or cotton. The reasons vary. Some people view leather as inappropriate for the workplace because it is too casual, some think it is too dressy, others think it is suggestive or sexual. To some, leather is perceived as a fad rather than a business staple.

11.

Caps, hats, and visors are acceptable in a casual workplace.

False. None of these are appropriate in any workplace, unless it is part of a uniform.

12.

Shoes should be the same color or darker than your skirt or pants.

True. You may think your shoes will not be noticed, but believe me, they will, especially if they stand out. Our eyes are drawn to the lightest area. If you wear dark pants and light shoes, your shoes will stand out. Shoes that are the same color or darker than your skirt or pants will not stand out or be distracting.

Chapter Summary

Remember:

✓ How you look and what you wear makes a statement about how you feel about yourself, your coworkers, and customers.

✓ Represent your company in the best possible manner. Every day, ask yourself, "What kind of impression do I want to make?" and select the clothing that will help you achieve your objective. Taking pride in your appearance shows that you take pride in yourself and your job.

✓ Dress better than you need to and dress for the position you want to have.

✓ You are always better off being slightly overdressed than underdressed. Even if your job doesn't require it, dress better than you need to. People will notice and may treat you differently as a result. More importantly, you will look as though you take yourself and your job seriously, and you may find that your appearance creates the perception that you are ready to move up to the next level.

✓ Pay attention to detail. Make sure your clothing fits well, is clean, and is in good condition.

✓ When it comes to clothing and appearance, little things make a big difference. You can spend a lot of money on a garment, but if it is too tight, stained, or the lining hangs out, it will be distracting and cheapen your look.

✓ Build a long-lasting wardrobe of classic styles and neutral colors.

✓ Be patient as you build your work wardrobe. Purchase quality clothing in basic, classic styles and colors. This will enable you to mix and match pieces in your wardrobe and to wear your clothing for years without worrying about anything going out of style.

✓ Change your look every now and then, whether it's a new hairstyle or shaving the beard you've grown. You need to look as though you know what you are doing, so as things evolve and change, make some personal changes as well.

Sticking with the same look for years will ultimately date you and people may question your competence.

✓ Wear a minimal amount of jewelry in the workplace. Accessories can add a nice touch to any outfit, but keep them to a minimum. You will want to have a nice watch and a few good pieces of jewelry, but remove any jewelry in uncommon places.

✓ Forgo fragrance or use it very sparingly. Remember that no smell is the best smell. Be sensitive to the many people who have allergies to perfumes, and keep in mind that although you can't smell the fragrance you put on, others can.

✓ Go to work dressed every day as if it were the first day of your job. Too many people become relaxed and place little importance on the very things that got them hired in the first place. Remember how much time you spent thinking about what to wear to your interview? Just because you have a job doesn't mean your appearance doesn't matter anymore. Put your best foot forward every single day.

Chapter 7

Communication Skills

Test Your Communication Skills

True or False?

1.

It's important to identify yourself when answering the phone, and the most professional greeting is to simply state your name.

2.

It isn't necessary to worry about punctuation, spelling, or grammar when using e-mail.

3.

Most people don't listen very well.

4.

In order to be a good conversationalist, you need to talk a lot.

5.

Always try to sit at the head of a table in a meeting because it is considered the power seat.

6.

All phone calls should be returned within one business day.

Test yourself as you read through this chapter. The answers appear on pages 188-189.

How Do You Sound to Others?

Have you ever heard yourself on an answering machine or listened to yourself on audiotape? What was your reaction? Most people are shocked and often react by saying, "That's not what I sound like!" We do sound differently to ourselves than we think we do.

The way you sound impacts your credibility and image. The following tips will help you to communicate clearly and sound pleasing to others:

Use appropriate grammar. You don't need to use big, impressive words to sound good to others. In fact, most people prefer simple language that is easy to understand. Avoid slang, jargon, and swearing, and if you feel it will help you, work on building your vocabulary and sentence structure.

Speak with a steady flow. When you speak, do your words flow? Or do you hem and haw, correct yourself, or undermine what you've said? The ability to think on your feet is an asset, so work on responding to questions and putting your thoughts together clearly.

Use good diction. If people frequently ask you to repeat yourself, you may not be communicating clearly. Make sure you enunciate and pronounce all words and sounds correctly, and avoid mumbling.

Eliminate excess verbiage. Using "ums" and "ahs" frequently in your conversation can be distracting to a listener. Try to speak clearly without using too many fillers.

Vary your inflection. If you vary your tone and inflection you will be more interesting to listen to. Avoid speaking in a monotone.

Add depth and confidence. You've probably heard people who "uptalk." They end every sentence "up," making their statements sound like questions. When this is done, people sound as though they are unsure about what they are saying. You are better off speaking in a slightly lower pitch than a higher one. Unless you are asking a question, don't end your sentences with "uptalk."

Watch your volume. There are situations when speaking loudly is an asset; for example, when you make a presentation to a large group or when you are in a noisy environment.

The way you sound impacts your credibility and image.

However, speaking too loudly in the wrong environment will be disruptive to others and is not recommended. If you speak too softly, people may not pay attention to what you have to say or may discount your credibility.

Express warmth. Pause before you answer a telephone call. Take a deep breath, if necessary, so that you sound welcoming to the caller. Avoid sounding rushed, irritated, or stressed.

Be aware of the emotional quality of your voice. You don't want to sound aggravated, stressed, or in a hurry when you are on the phone. Avoid speaking too fast, too slow, too loud, or too soft.

Telephone Techniques

The telephone is a viable business tool, and using it effectively is essential to your success. There is more to using the telephone than picking it up to answer or dial out. Although the person on the other end cannot see you, your image still comes through during your telephone exchanges. When you interact with someone face to face, what you say is supported by your facial expressions and body language, which help clarify, support, and add interest to your words. On the telephone, the only way to enhance your words is by sounding animated and interesting. You can achieve this through your tone and inflection. Think about the broadcasters you hear on the radio. Although you can't see them, you can sense by listening whether someone is actively involved or passionate about what they are saying. Imagine how boring it would be to listen to a broadcaster who spoke without using any vocal variety and spoke in a monotone for the entire broadcast.

The telephone is a viable business tool, and using it effectively is essential to your success.

Smile while you speak on the phone, and if you really want to add impact, try standing as you speak. This will add strength and energy to your voice. You may want to place a mirror by your phone as a reminder to express yourself in an energetic and lively manner.

Hold That Hold Button

Do you like being placed on hold? Most people don't, and when on hold, seconds seem like minutes. If you must place someone on hold, never leave the caller for more than 30 seconds without coming back and asking permission to put them on hold longer. Always ask permission anytime you want to place someone on hold. Don't ever assume it is all right unless you've asked and waited for a reply.

I was doing a radio interview by telephone about casual dress. The interview wasn't going very well. It was apparent that the person interviewing me hadn't done any preparation, and she was having a difficult time getting into the conversation. Apparently, she thought that *I* was the problem, and when she put me on hold, she didn't press the right button because I heard her tell her producer, "This woman is really boring, let's get rid of her."

I was dumfounded. I've been called many things, but *boring* has never been one of them! I couldn't believe she said that! Be careful about what you say when you *think* someone is on hold, be sure that you really do press the hold button. And always thank the person for holding when you return. Be sure to return quickly. Leaving someone on hold longer than 20 to 30 seconds is not a good idea and can make the person feel as though he or she has been forgotten.

Call waiting or a second phone line is great for those occasions in which you simply cannot miss a call, but most people use them for much more than an urgent situation. If you are talking with someone and another call comes in and you put the first caller on hold, you are placing more importance on the new caller than the person with whom you are talking.

Placing someone on hold is an inconvenience to that person. It does not show respect for their time. When you ignore call waiting, you make the person you are talking to your top priority, which should be your objective.

Answering and Placing Calls

When the telephone rings, try to answer it by the third ring or have it go to voice mail. No one likes to wait for five, 10, or 15 rings to get to talk to someone. The manner in which you answer the phone is both a reflection on your professionalism and your company. Find out if your company suggests answering the phone a particular way. If your company does not have a preferred greeting, you will need to decide how you will answer the phone.

When calls come directly to you, and you know they are either internal or from a personal acquaintance, you can answer more casually than when answering calls from people outside the company. It is always important to state your name when answering the phone. For internal calls, stating your first name is usually sufficient, but when answering calls that come directly to you from customers or others outside the company, you should use your first and last name. Here are a few suggestions on how to respond to incoming calls:

Internal or personal callers

"This is John" or "John Johnson speaking" will suffice, but it doesn't hurt to add a touch of friendliness by saying, "Hello, this is John."

Outside callers

"Good morning, ABC Company, this is Anne Smith."

It is important to identify yourself when making an outbound call, too. Unless you know the person you are calling quite well, use both your first and last name along with your company name.

"Hi Jan, this is Meg Tate with Arthur Investments calling."

When a receptionist or assistant answers a call, always identify yourself:

"Good morning, this is Meg Tate with Arthur Investments calling. Is Marc Jones available?"

Keep in mind that most people are inundated with phone calls every day. When you call someone, you are interrupting him or her and calling at your convenience, not necessarily a convenient time for that person.

Chances are you won't always reach the person you are calling and may find yourself in rounds of telephone tag with many people. You may find that you will be most successful in reaching people if you call first thing in the morning or late in the day. If you want to reach someone, it is your responsibility to continue to call until you do.

Voice Mail

You can accomplish quite a bit through voice mail, often without ever talking directly with someone. Learn to use voice mail to set lunch dates, meetings, and appointments and to get answers to your questions.

When leaving a voice mail message for someone, keep in mind that your message is one of many the person you are calling will be receiving that day. Make your message brief and to the point. It is most helpful to write out the main points you want to cover so that you don't waste your time trying to decide what to say as you are recording.

It is a good idea to leave your telephone number both at the beginning and end of a message. This way, you can be sure the person has the number and it enables the receiver to ensure that he or she has written it correctly. When you leave your name and number, speak s-l-o-w-l-y. I can't tell you the number of times I have had difficulty writing down a number that has been left on my voice mail because the person said it so quickly.

One way to be sure you are saying the number slowly enough is to write it down as you say it.

If you are struggling to reach someone, try to set a specific time for the two of you to talk. I find this works quite well. Leave a few options of times you will be available.

If you have left several messages and have not received a return call, you need to evaluate the situation. There does come a point when you risk becoming a pest. If you've left several messages and attempted to reach someone and are getting no response, you should realize that the lack of a response is a response. The silence is telling you that the person is not interested. You may want to leave one final message, stating that it is the last time you will call for awhile. Be pleasant and leave the door open to future connections. It's important to know when to walk away.

Many people update and change their voice mail daily. If you choose to do this, be sure you remember to change it each

If you want to reach someone, it is your responsibility to continue to call until you do.

---

day. I've called people whose voice mail messages are weeks old. Hearing "I'll be out of the office until March 30" when it is April 15 does not send the right message to the caller.

Listen to your message before you use it to make sure you are pleased with the way it sounds. Try to sound upbeat and avoid a monotone delivery. If you say you will get back to the caller as soon as possible, then do it! When you fail to return a call, basically you are telling that person (by your silence), "I don't care about you" or "You're not important enough for me to call."

Words Send a Message

The words you use when speaking are important in all business communication, but even more important over the phone. Avoid slang, as it sounds too casual and youthful. Answering with a "Yo" or "Hey" is too casual. So is telling someone to "Hang on," instead of asking him or her to hold for a moment. Rather than saying, "How ya doin?" say, "How are you doing?"

Always end a conversation by thanking the person for their time, and saying good-bye. Avoid phrases such as "Ba-bye" or "Talk to ya later."

If you answer a call for a coworker who is unavailable, there is no need to give a detailed description as to why the person can't come to the phone. Don't announce that someone is in the restroom or taking a cigarette break. Simply state that the person is unavailable or has stepped away from his or her workspace for a moment.

Speaking on Speakerphones

No one likes to have a phone on their ear or shoulder all day, which is why headsets and speakerphones are nice alternatives. The only danger with speakerphones is that the voice of the person on the other end is amplified and can be heard by anyone who happens to be nearby. Therefore, if you are listening to your messages on a speakerphone, be aware of other people overhearing what is being said.

Some people prefer to answer calls by pressing the speakerphone button, but it is better to answer the phone directly and ask permission to put the person on the speakerphone. No one likes to be placed on a speakerphone unknowingly, and

Telephone Dos

- Establish a professional way to answer your phone.
- Identify yourself with your first and last names and company name.
- Smile when you talk on the phone.
- Ask the person you've called if it is a convenient time to talk.
- State the purpose for your call at the beginning of the conversation.
- Keep your conversations short and to the point.
- Give verbal feedback.
- Pay full attention to the person on the phone.
- Ask permission to place someone on hold.
- Thank the person for holding.
- Return all calls within one business day.
- Change your voice mail message daily or as needed.
- Answer your phone by the third ring.
- Speak courteously to everyone when calling a business, including the receptionist.
- Avoid outside distractions.

some people find it offensive, feeling as though you are too busy to take the time to pick up the phone to talk with them. The impression is that you may be doing other things as you are talking on the phone. Beware: the sound of hitting keys on your computer is amplified through the speakerphone, as are opening drawers and shuffling through papers.

It may be necessary to use a speakerphone when bringing together several people, but the same protocol applies. Begin the conversation through the mouthpiece and then ask each person to be included in the conversation for permission to turn on the speakerphone.

Telephone Don'ts

✗ Eat, smoke, or chew gum while on the phone.

✗ Type on your computer or rustle through paper while talking to someone.

✗ Use the speakerphone without asking permission of the person you are talking with.

✗ Take calls when you are with someone else.

✗ Place someone on hold for more than 30 seconds.

✗ Say you will return a call if you won't.

✗ Engage in idle chitchat.

✗ Screen calls.

✗ Use slang or profanity.

✗ Forget to update your voice mail message.

✗ Talk with someone else while on the phone.

✗ Yawn, sigh, or breathe too loudly.

You also need to inform the person on the other end of the phone that this is a group call. Identify the persons in the room and allow each person to say hello after being introduced. Then begin the conversation. It can be tricky to have a conference call this way, but it can be very effective if done properly. If you are one of many in a room, always announce your name before speaking to identify yourself so the person receiving the call knows who is speaking.

Pagers and Cellular Phones

It is a great convenience to be able to reach anyone, anytime, anywhere. It can also be intrusive and inconvenient. The ability to retreat and get away from everything (including the office) is becoming more and more difficult.

There are certain places and occasions in which you should turn your phone and pagers *off.* Anytime you are a part of an audience, whether at a movie, play, or concert, listening to a speaker, in a meeting, or at a wedding or funeral, a ringing or beeping sound will be a distraction and an interruption. There is nothing as embarrassing as having all eyes on you as you struggle to answer or turn off your phone or pager.

If there is some urgent or pressing reason you simply cannot wait until a break or intermission to check messages, then put your phone or pager on vibrate. Let it interrupt *you,* but there is no reason it needs to disturb everyone else.

When you are out for a meal, the same rule applies. If you take a call and ignore the person you are with, leaving him or her with nothing to do, the implied message is that the caller is more important than the person you are with.

If someone needs to reach you, they will reach you. Most calls can wait an hour or so. Be respectful and courteous of others and focus on the people you are with by turning your pager or phone off.

Another annoyance occurs when people have conversations on cellular phones that can be heard by everyone around them. Be discreet as to where you have your conversations and what you talk about. Most people don't want or need to know about the intimate details of your life, which are often discussed on the phone.

I was in a restroom and heard a woman engaged in a conversation on her phone. Toilets were flushing, people were coming and going, and she was in a stall having a typical conversation. I couldn't believe it! A restroom is one of the most inappropriate places to talk on the phone.

In addition, be careful about talking on the phone while driving. This distracts you from your driving and decreases your ability to react quickly. Using a headphone will free your hands and is a good idea if you must talk and drive.

Almost 50 percent of major U.S. employers store and retrieve employee e-mail. Sixty-three percent monitor Internet use.

Source: American Management Association

E-Mail Etiquette

The World Wide Web and e-mail have changed the way we do business. Efficient and effective, e-mail allows us to reach people and conduct business much faster than regular mail. Many people prefer to use e-mail to communicate instead of the telephone.

I received a question for my column from a reader who wondered how formally e-mail must be written. The reader assumed that e-mail was designed for efficiency and ease and didn't worry much about sending formal or structured e-mail. He didn't usually start with a "Dear John" or end with

"Sincerely yours." Instead, he would cut and paste bits of information into his e-mail and send it without checking for spelling and grammar errors.

It wasn't until one of his friends told him that he was offended by his e-mail style that he began to wonder about it. His friend informed him that he expected to be greeted at the start of all correspondence and that he should read through his e-mails before he sent them to ensure that they were coherent and to the point.

I opened the topic up to all of my readers and asked their opinions on the subject. My readers were divided on this issue. Half felt as my writer did, that e-mail was meant to be fast and convenient, and that there was no need to worry about format or structure.

The other half felt that e-mail was the same as any type of business correspondence and that all letters should be written in a business format with correct spelling and punctuation.

I concluded that, at the risk of offending someone, you should never *assume* it is fine to be too casual in your correspondence. Begin all e-mail correspondence as you would any other type of correspondence. As you build a relationship with a person, take note of the manner in which he or she communicates with you and follow his or her lead. This is the safest way to ensure you won't offend anyone.

However, even if someone sends you an e-mail with many mistakes, it doesn't mean you should do the same. Remember, e-mail can be saved, printed, and distributed. Before you press the send button, be sure that what you are sending reflects positively on you and your company.

Some of the e-mail slang and abbreviations you may use with friends may not be viewed favorably in the business world. Smiley faces have become one way to add some feeling to an e-mail, but they shouldn't be included in any business e-mail you send unless someone has sent you a smiley face first and you want to reciprocate.

Keep in mind that people are inundated with e-mail messages. E-mail is fast and easy, and readers are looking for fast and easy ways to delete messages and get through their mail.

Remember, e-mail can be saved, printed, and distributed. Before you press the send button, be sure that what you are sending reflects positively on you and your company.

You Will Maximize
Your E-mail Efficiency if you:

• Write an effective, attention grabbing subject line.

• Keep it short (most people won't scroll all the way down to read an entire e-mail).

• Write in a 10- or 12-point size.

• Do not write in all CAPS; it is the equivalent of SHOUTING at someone.

• Use spell check.

• Use professional greetings and salutations.

• Include your name, company name, title, address, and telephone number in your signature block.

• Check your e-mail frequently and respond quickly.

• Do not forward jokes, poems, or special promotions unless requested.

• Send important documents by regular mail, too.

• Keep your sentences short.

• Use a professional, businesslike tone.

• Avoid sending personal letters or information.

Surfing the Internet

You will, undoubtedly, have access to the World Wide Web through your computer at work. While this computer and the Internet are provided to you for business use, many companies allow their employees to use both for personal use as well, and some provide laptops to be taken home.

Keep in mind that computer technology is very sophisticated. Wherever you go and whatever you do on the World

Wide Web will be known by your company. Therefore, think twice about where you go on the Internet.

Although most people use the Internet and their computers wisely, others take advantage and spend valuable work time surfing the Net. If you choose to do this, it is just a matter of time before someone catches on to you. Chances are either your work will suffer or you will. Use the Internet wisely and don't take advantage of having it at your fingertips.

Small Talk: A Big Subject

Every day you will find yourself greeting many different people. You'll see the receptionist, coworkers, people in the hall, on the elevator, at the coffee stop, and in the cafeteria. You will smile and acknowledge many of these people quite frequently, but what will you say after you say hello?

Your ability to carry on a conversation and put people at ease is crucial to your success. It can be awkward to sit next to someone in silence as you wait for a meeting to begin.

Making small talk is an art, but anyone can develop good conversational skills. If you are sincerely interested in other people, you are already on your way to becoming a good conversationalist.

Many people assume they need to talk a lot in order to be interesting, but talking a lot isn't something you need to do. One time I was at an event and sat next to a very interesting man, who had lots to say about his experiences and travels. I asked him questions and encouraged him to tell me about himself. He obliged, and by the end of the evening as we said good-bye, he told me how much he enjoyed talking with me. I didn't say much, but he *perceived* me to be a great conversationalist because I was able to get him talking.

People love to talk about themselves, and if you have a sincere interest in others, they will love being around you. People who talk too much are often shunned or viewed negatively.

People will perceive you to be a great conversationalist if you develop ease in drawing people out. All you need to do is ask the right questions, listen, and give some feedback. You

Wherever you go and whatever you do on the World Wide Web will be known by your company. Therefore, think twice about where you go on the Internet.

need to know the difference between asking a question that leads to a conversation, and a question that leads nowhere or alienates the other person. These types of questions are called *conversation starters* and *conversation stoppers,* respectively.

To generate a conversation, you need to establish a common ground with someone. You want to give people a reason to talk with you. This can be difficult to do when you have just met someone, but by asking the right questions and picking a safe topic, you should be able to lead and develop a conversation with almost anyone.

Conversation Starters

The following conversation starters are generally not controversial and are neutral topics that should enable you to establish rapport with anyone and carry on a conversation:

- The weather
- Sports
- Current events
- Food/restaurants
- Entertainment
- Movies
- Books
- Vacations/travel
- Family
- Work
- Hobbies

Here's how a conversation might progress:

Eric: How long have you been working here?

Kim: I've been here for five years.

Eric: That's great! What department do you work in?

Kim: I'm in advertising.

Eric: Really? How did you get into advertising?

Kim: I studied it in school and then worked one summer for an advertising agency and really enjoyed it.

Eric: So what school did you go to?

Notice that Eric didn't stop after one question, but continued to probe and appear interested. However, Eric would be better off asking questions that require more than a yes or no response. Notice how he finally gets Kim to talk more.

Kim: I went to the University of Minnesota

Eric: No kidding! My best friend is from Minnesota. He always tells me how cold the winters are. In fact, when I visited him it was something like 20 below zero! How did you deal with the weather?

Kim: Well, I'll tell you, it was a real shock to my system. I'm from the South, and we considered it a cold day when it was 50 degrees! I heard it was cold but had no idea how cold it could get. Where in Minnesota does your friend live?

In this conversation, Eric contributed to the conversation, shared some information, and then turned the conversation back over to Kim. A give and take is the best kind of conversation. If Kim is astute, she should ask Eric questions about himself, too, which she finally did. Eric listened to and acknowledged what Kim said and continued to show interest by asking more questions.

Asking open-ended questions will increase your chances of getting a *response,* rather than an *answer* from someone. For example, the following are examples of effective and ineffective conversation starters:

Open-ended question:
How did you get into this line of work?

This question requires a response. By asking open-ended questions, you increase your chance of carrying on a conversation with someone.

Closed question:
You work in the accounting department, don't you?

This question requires a simple yes or no answer and will not lead to a conversation very easily.

As long as you are sincere, and not nosy, your questions should lead into a conversation. And, it is fine to interject some of your experiences as well.

Conversation Stoppers

Conversation stoppers are questions or comments that fail to lead to further discussion and basically bring you to a dead end. Refrain from asking personal questions or from appearing nosy or intrusive. Some topics are riskier than others. You are wise to stay away from asking questions or talking about:

- Personal finances/money
- Romance/relationships
- Sex
- Politics
- Religion
- Weight/diets
- Divorce
- Illness/death
- Other people/gossip
- Controversial subjects
- Personal problems

For example, beginning a conversation with "I feel lousy today, I wonder if I am getting the flu" will push people away from you. No one wants to hear your complaints, and no one wants to catch what you've got.

Talking with Supervisors and Superiors

Once you feel you have the ability to talk with people and put them at ease, you will undoubtedly feel more comfortable meeting new people at social and business events. However, even great conversationalists can become tongue-tied when face to face with someone of a higher status, in particular, the boss or head of the company.

Feeling a bit self-conscious or nervous is quite common when talking with a superior, but it doesn't have to be that way. It may help to realize that your supervisor is just as uncomfortable as you are in certain situations. Even the president of the company can feel awkward due to his or her position and long to fit in with everyone else.

Feeling a bit self-conscious or nervous is quite common when talking with a superior, but it doesn't have to be that way.

Treat your superiors as people. Show them the same interest and respect you show others. When you find yourself standing with or sitting by a superior, use the opportunity to make small talk. Don't try to cover big issues or problems in this setting, and don't use the opportunity to brag about your accomplishments or ask for a raise.

Talking with Coworkers and Customers

I was sitting in the beautiful lobby of an insurance company waiting to meet with someone. It was shortly after the noon hour and the lobby was busy with people coming and going. Two women stood in the middle of the lobby, and although I wasn't trying to eavesdrop, I couldn't help but overhear their conversation. Once I realized what they were talking about, I was shocked. Apparently, one of the women had some health problems and had been to the doctor the previous day. I can understand how she might want to share the information with her friend, but talking loudly about every detail of it in the middle of the lobby during the noon hour was inappropriate.

Don't get involved in discussions about other people, and don't be the bearer of gossip about anyone.

You will undoubtedly become friendly with the people you work with and develop a comfort level with them. You will see these people daily and probably share many details of your life with them. However, there are boundaries in the workplace, and it is important to recognize what they are because no one may ever tell you.

Casual conversation with coworkers will help build relationships. You will probably find yourself asking coworkers how their weekend was, about their children, their house, and other safe topics. You may develop closer friendships with some people, and that is fine, but save the private and personal conversations for after hours away from the office.

It's fine to ask someone how they are feeling and to discuss health a bit, but avoid getting into too much detail. You also want to avoid detailed discussions in the presence of others about anything that is of a personal nature.

Gossip is an inevitable part of human interactions, and you will hear gossip in your workplace. Don't get involved in discussions about other people, and don't be the bearer of gossip about anyone. Avoid complaining about things or other people. If you have a problem with someone, go to the source.

There is little, if any, privacy in most workplaces. Be cognizant of your surroundings and keep your conversations light and businesslike.

Learn to Listen

Once you've developed good conversational skills and the ability to draw people out, be sure you really listen to what is being said. Have you ever been talking to someone on the phone and felt as though you weren't being heard? Perhaps the person you were talking with was watching television, reading, or doing something at the same time he or she was supposed to be listening to you.

Good listening skills need to be reinforced consistently.

It is important to listen to someone when they are talking. When you do, you will have fewer misunderstandings and people will appreciate that you care about what they have to say. Read through the following questions and assess your listening skills by recording the number of yes and no responses you have.

Do You . . .
- Think you are a good listener?
- Ask questions?
- Avoid interrupting when someone is speaking?
- Show interest by nodding and leaning forward?
- Give feedback by reacting to what is said with an occasional "uh-huh" or the like?
- Avoid outside distractions?
- Maintain eye contact by looking at the person who is talking?
- Ask for clarification if you don't understand what is being said?
- Refrain from finishing other people's sentences?

If you answered yes to most of the questions, you are on your way to becoming a great listener. Good listening skills need to be reinforced constantly. There are so many ways in which we can become distracted, which makes listening a challenge.

Studies have shown that most of us only retain about 25 percent of what we hear; this means we miss 75 percent of what is communicated! We can all work on our listening skills.

Focus is the key, so don't try to do two or more things at once. If you are talking with someone and the phone rings, let it go to voice mail. If you see someone walking by, avoid watching and remain focused on the person you are with.

Glancing at your watch is fine if you do it once in awhile, but looking at it frequently sends a negative message to the person you are with. Your glance is a signal that time may be running out. This can be useful when you need to let someone know you are short on time. But looking at your watch too frequently might suggest that you are bored, impatient, or disinterested.

Looking at the person you are talking with, leaning forward slightly, and giving feedback by paraphrasing what is said are excellent ways to enhance your listening skills.

Managing Meetings

If you work in a company, chances are that you will be required to attend meetings. As you take on more responsibility, the number of meetings you must attend may increase. Some people feel that too many meetings are a waste of time. If you are responsible for holding a meeting, be sensitive to the fact that you are taking people away from other important things they could be doing.

If you are responsible for holding a meeting, be sensitive to the fact that you are taking people away from other important things they could be doing.

Meetings are most effective when they are brief and to the point. An agenda is always recommended, along with a specific starting and ending time.

Where you sit will impact your involvement. The most powerful place to sit is at the head of the table facing the door, which allows you to see who is coming and going. The head of the table is usually reserved for the meeting leader.

The middle of the table is considered one of the best places to sit, and sitting next to the leader is also a great place to be.

Even more important than where you sit is how you act and react during a meeting. Meetings are most effective when

Tips For Effective Meetings

- Arrive on time.
- Greet everyone.
- Have writing implements with you.
- Bring your calendar with you (in the event future meetings are planned).
- Sit upright.
- Focus on the person who is speaking.
- Avoid side conversations with others.
- Wait to speak until others have finished.
- Keep your comments brief.
- Avoid changing or straying away from the subject being discussed.
- When asked to participate, get involved.
- Avoid making negative facial expressions or sounds (rolling the eyes, sighing).
- Avoid yawning.
- Turn your phone, pager, and all alarms off.
- Come prepared.
- Avoid any distractions.
- Give your full attention to the speaker.
- When you speak, speak clearly, loudly, and confidently.

everyone is involved. However, there is a time to sit back and listen and a time to contribute. Let the facilitator dictate the flow of the meeting.

Be aware of and control your body language and facial expressions, and make sure you appear interested and involved.

Test Your Communication Skills

Questions and Answers

True or False?

1.

It's important to identify yourself when answering the phone, and the most professional greeting is to simply state your name.

False. It is true that it is important to identify yourself, but simply stating your name can sound abrupt. It is a good idea to use some type of salutation along with both your name and company name.

2.

It isn't necessary to worry about punctuation, spelling, or grammar when using e-mail.

False. Using e-mail in business should be viewed differently from personal e-mail. All written business communication should be composed in a professional manner, which includes proper punctuation, spelling, and grammar. Many e-mail messages are saved and printed. You never know who might see your message, and you want to be represented in the best possible manner through all written documents.

3.

Most people don't listen very well.

True. Studies have found that most of us miss three-fourths of what is said to us. By adapting better listening skills you will become more efficient and spend less time dealing with misunderstandings.

4.

In order to be a good conversationalist, you need to talk a lot.

False. People who talk too much can become a nuisance and are often viewed as either insecure or insensitive. To truly converse with someone, there needs to be an exchange of ideas, which includes both points of view.

5.

Always try to sit at the head of a table in a meeting because it is considered the power seat.

False. The head of the table is the power seat but should be reserved for the person(s) leading the meeting. Don't be the first to sit down, and when in a large meeting, sit toward the front rather than the back of a room.

6.

All phone calls should be returned within one business day.

True. The longer you wait to return a call, the louder the message is that you don't care or don't value that person. When a call is important to you, find the time to return it. Make it a practice to return all calls within one business day.

Chapter Summary

Remember:

✓ Although you can't be seen when on the telephone, your attitude and personality come through. Keep a mirror by your phone to remind you that through your voice, you can be "seen."

✓ Pay attention to the way you sound to others. Pause before you answer the phone or place a call so that you come across as friendly and in control.

✓ The telephone is one of the best business tools you have. Use it wisely, and remember, a phone call to someone is an interruption to them. Always have a purpose for your call and keep your conversations short and to the point.

✓ Update your outgoing voice mail message frequently, and when leaving messages for others, keep them brief. Always include your name and telephone number at the beginning and end of any message you leave.

✓ Limit your use of your personal, cellular phone in public and watch your conversation; you never know who may be listening.

✓ Become a great conversationalist by becoming interested in others.

✓ Learn to listen; you have two ears and one mouth, use them proportionately.

✓ Arrive at all meetings on time, greet everyone you see, and be prepared to participate.

Chapter 8

Customer Service

Test Your Customer Service Skills

True or False?

1.

Most customers won't tell you when they are dissatisfied.

2.

One of the best ways to deal with an upset customer is by listening.

3.

One word a customer never wants to hear is *no.*

4.

An angry customer is likely to tell three to five other people about his or her experience.

5.

Rules should never be broken.

6.

Coworkers should be considered customers, too.

7.

Always thank a customer at the end of a transaction or conversation.

Test yourself as you read through this chapter. The answers appear on pages 208-210.

Setting the Tone

It was a beautiful summer evening and my family and I decided to stop by a neighborhood restaurant for something to eat on our way home from a movie. It was 9:00 PM and we hadn't had dinner yet, so we were hungry. As we pulled into the parking lot, we were relieved to see that there weren't too many cars and assumed we would be seated and served right away.

We entered the restaurant and were greeted by the hostess, a young woman I recognized from our frequent visits to the restaurant. I greeted her with a friendly hello, but instead of smiling or saying hello in return, she allowed our conversation to proceed like this:

Me: Hi!

Hostess: How many?

Me: Five

Hostess: Smoking or non?

Me: Non

We certainly didn't make much of a connection, and I could instantly tell that she was not in a good mood. In fact, I felt as though we had irritated her by walking through the door.

The hostess had an opportunity to develop a rapport with us. She could have welcomed us to the restaurant, told us about the food specials, or simply asked us how we were doing. Instead, she had me mumbling one-word phrases to her.

The hostess then told us that we would have to wait to be seated. I looked around the restaurant and saw a number of empty tables. When I asked her about the empty seats, she informed me that they were short-staffed and had to space the seating. I began to understand why the parking lot was empty. I wondered what the service would be like once we did sit down. All I needed was a little reassurance, but I wasn't getting any. I began to feel like an unwanted intruder because she seemed perturbed that I was questioning her about the wait. When we finally were seated, the hostess never apologized for the delay. She didn't thank us for waiting or wish us a nice meal. I concluded that she didn't care or that perhaps she didn't like us.

I realized that our entire experience would have been different had she managed to greet us with a smile and a hello. Anyone who greets customers should begin all encounters with some type of greeting. Customers are your *guests* and they deserve to be treated as such. Welcoming your guests is the easiest way to set the right tone.

Perhaps you've had experience providing a service. You may have worked in a retail store or a restaurant or cut grass or shoveled snow for neighbors. If you haven't had experience providing service, you have most likely had experience as a customer.

As a customer, can you think of times you've had a great experience? What made it memorable? And, if there were times when service was bad, how did you feel as a result?

There have been times when I've entered an establishment as a customer and felt as though I were invisible because no one acknowledged me. There I was, a live person ready to spend money, but the clerk was more interested in cleaning, counting the day's receipts, or talking with coworkers.

In that instant, a negative tone was set. And once that tone is set, it doesn't usually change. From that first moment, based on the way I am greeted (or not greeted), I've been able to determine what kind of service I will receive—and I've rarely been wrong in my initial assumptions.

Anyone who greets customers should begin all encounters with some type of greeting. Customers are your guests *and they deserve to be treated as such.*

Every Business Has Customers

No matter what industry you are in or what job you have, you will have customers that need to be served. In fact, 79 percent of Americans work in a service industry, according to Petra Marquart, author of *The Power of Service: Keeping Customers for Life* (Ponderosa Press, 1998).

As a customer, you have expectations. You expect to be treated fairly and courteously and to get what you pay for. When we receive more than we expect, we are delighted. When we receive less than we expect, we are more than disappointed: we are often outraged.

We love getting a bargain, but if we perceive we have been cheated in any way (which includes poor service), we feel as though something has been stolen from us.

In addition to its external customers, a company has internal customers. You may provide a service for other people in your company or work with other departments. Everyone you deal with deserves to be treated well.

Challenges of Customer Service

I realize that despite a worker's best intentions, sometimes circumstances can make it difficult to provide good service. I've discussed the perils of customer service a number of times in my newspaper column, and I received the following letter as a response to one of those discussions:

> Dear Sue,
>
> I've worked for several years at a bank, where service quality has been severely (and intentionally) hurt by employee cutbacks and various other efforts directed at increasing profits.
>
> The emphasis used to be on customer quality (putting the customer first) and doing your job quickly and efficiently, but now the emphasis has shifted to using the few employees remaining to pick up the slack while trying to service the customers.
>
> Corporate executives explicitly told us that we were going to have to change our mindset away from customer service, and toward efficiency instead. The company has told us that our priority should be on increasing profits for the shareholders, which has resulted in a decline in the quality of service for the few customers we have left as well as a demoralized and overworked group of people.
>
> Management used to be concerned with long lines and making people wait, but now people routinely wait in line to see a teller or account representative as long as 15 minutes. It isn't always the fault of the employee when service is poor. Often, we just can't help it, because there aren't enough employees or resources. It just seems as though people don't care about making the customer #1 anymore.
>
> Signed,
> Realist

Here is my response as it appeared in my column:

Dear Realist,
You understand the reality of the situation, now make the decision to move forward. With all of the cutbacks, you still have a job and should be grateful for that. Provide the best service you can and make a commitment to have a positive impact on the people you work with and the customers you serve.

I must admit that my response was a little harsh. You see, the day I wrote that response, I was feeling a little under the weather. When it appeared in the paper the following week, even I was a bit surprised at the tone of my response, but I was unprepared for the outcry from my readers.

I was inundated with responses, some of which were downright nasty. Service providers accused me of being clueless and unsympathetic toward retail clerks. One man wrote me a very harsh five-page letter telling me that I should quit my job because I was out of touch. Although most of the people who wrote to me were angry at my response, there were a few who praised me for encouraging personal responsibility.

I was concerned that I had let my readers down. I thought I might have goofed, so I was prepared to apologize and change my advice. Several weeks later, I addressed the issue again in another column:

Dear Readers,
Because many of you who took the time to call or write were not in agreement with my response to "Realist," the service provider who was having a difficult time providing good service, I read the question over and over to see if I missed something. But after reviewing it, as much as I wanted to find another solution and change my answer, I couldn't.

Sure I could have been more sympathetic and focused on the challenges workers face. I could have suggested that the employee leave the bank and look for work where customers are valued more than the bottom line. I could have asked you, my readers, what advice you would give this person. But I didn't. What I did do was give "Realist" the only positive and proactive advice I could think of, and that was to take control of what she could and give the best service possible.

"Realist" is working under difficult circumstances. If the concerns have been discussed with management, then at some point the only options left are to accept things as they are or leave.

If "Realist" chooses to stay, the only positive thing to do is to make the best of a difficult situation. We can't change or control the actions of others, but we can change and control our reaction to them.

Some of you look to me for validation and others hope for a new perspective. I know the workplace can be a nasty place. It can also be a wonderful place to learn and grow, both personally and professionally. Ultimately, the way we view our workplace, the choices we make, and the way we treat our customers is entirely up to each one of us.

Again, I received many responses, but this time, more were in support of my advice than against it. It is true, everyone who works in a service position has a *personal responsibility* to provide the best service he or she can.

When I entered the restaurant that night with my family and encountered the unhappy hostess who greeted me by saying, "How many?" I knew instantly by the hostess's words, facial expression, and attitude that she was not pleased that we walked through that door. I can jump to many different conclusions as to why. She mentioned they were short-staffed, so she probably had to work extra hard and deal with problems that night. It was already 9:00 PM, and she may have been hoping the customers would stop coming so she could leave early. Maybe she had an unhappy encounter with her boss or a customer and was feeling bad about that.

Whatever the reason for her attitude, it shouldn't be *my* problem. After all, I am the *customer* and should have been *welcomed* into the restaurant, not treated as an intruder. As service professionals, we all need to find ways to manage the stress and problems that will always be a part of our work experience.

When people come to you and want to pay you money for something in return, they expect to get what they pay for and *more*: they want service with a smile.

Everyone who works in a service position has a personal responsibility to provide the best service he or she can.

Complaints Can Be Helpful

Any business that deals with the public needs to provide outstanding customer service in order to keep loyal and satisfied customers. Companies that hear few complaints may think things are fine, but often they are wrong. In fact, 96 percent of dissatisfied customers never complain about rude or discourteous treatment, according to Petra Marquart. However, each unhappy customer will tell 14 to 20 other people about their negative experience.

Any business that deals with the public needs to provide outstanding customer service in order to keep loyal and satisfied customers.

For every one complaint that a company receives, there are dozens of others they never even hear about. And just hearing from customers doesn't mean the problem is solved. How customers are treated as they move through the complaint process will determine whether the resolution is positive or simply another failure.

Feel fortunate when a customer complains, because it is valuable feedback. As painful as it may be, it is better said to *you* than to 14 or more other people.

Problems Are Inevitable

Customer Disservice

A few years ago, I was in Chicago for a seminar. I was exhausted after a long day and was happy when I got to my hotel room. I had an important seminar to present the next day and needed to get some rest. I was tired and hungry, so I ordered room service. I attempted to turn on the television to help me relax before I went over the notes for my presentation. It didn't work. I called the front desk and was told that someone would be right up to check things out. Fifteen minutes went by, and there was still no response. I called again, this time even more frustrated.

Finally, someone came and checked out the television only to discover it couldn't be repaired that night. I didn't feel I should have to be without a working television, so I packed my things and moved to a new room. Once I was settled, my food was cold, so they sent up a new meal.

As I was about to unwind, the phone rang. It was another guest in the hotel who was trying to place a long-distance call but was reaching my room instead. This happened repeatedly. Again I called the front desk, this time quite irritated. "Look," I said, "I came to your hotel to relax and have had nothing but aggravation since I checked in. I have a very important meeting tomorrow and need to prepare, then get to sleep. I have been so busy changing rooms and dealing with problems that I haven't had a chance to eat my dinner, do my work, or get any rest."

The lack of empathy and indifferent response I received from the front desk clerk was making matters worse. All I needed was to find someone who could help me get my needs met. In fact, I *craved* some compassion.

I finally asked to speak to the manager. After an unusually long period of time, the manager finally called. After listening carefully to my story, she not only apologized but was as appalled as I was and seemed to completely understand how frustrated I was. This in itself was very comforting. In fact, once she validated my feelings, I was satisfied, and the more she sided with me, the more I found myself defending her and her employees.

She told me she wasn't going to charge me for the room, and offered me a complimentary breakfast the next morning and an upgrade on my room for my next visit. She did more than I ever expected or needed to make up for my inconvenience.

Do you think I stayed at that hotel again? You bet I did. In fact, I was in Chicago every month the following year and stayed there every visit. I became a VIP customer. That hotel reaped the rewards of handling a service problem effectively. As customers, we need to know that our complaints are understood and taken seriously, and this manager knew that very well.

Problems are inevitable. Don't become anxious when someone complains to you. Be appreciative. Anytime anyone gives you feedback, whether good or bad, you are learning something extremely valuable—your customer's opinion. As in any relationship, there will be good and bad days, and there will always be a need to communicate. Be open to what some-one has to say. Listen to the problem, because many times that is all it takes to satisfy an upset customer. Then make an

> *Anytime anyone gives you feedback, whether good or bad, you are learning something extremely valuable—your customer's opinion.*

attempt to do something about the problem. Take the complaint personally and make solving it your responsibility. Anytime a customer is belligerent or out of control, you should get someone to assist you.

If you don't know what to offer as a solution, try asking the customer what he or she wants. You may be surprised to learn that most customers don't want to take advantage of you; they just want what is reasonable.

How Not to Perform Customer Service

I don't feel I am especially difficult to please as a customer, but I am probably more likely than most to stand up for what I feel I deserve. So when I ordered a phone through my telephone company but got the wrong product, I didn't hesitate to call and let the phone company know. The problem was that the company's customer service representative (CSR) couldn't find a record of a phone being sent to me. After numerous calls, I couldn't find anyone who would send me a return label since they had no record of the phone, so I put the phone away (because I couldn't use it) and forgot about it. I figured that as long as I wasn't being charged for it, if they didn't want it back, it wasn't my problem.

About six months later, I noticed a charge I couldn't account for on my phone bill. When I called to investigate, I was told the charge was for the telephone I had received. I couldn't believe it! I told my story about how I tried to return the phone, and that since I never used it, I would like to send it back. The CSR told me that I couldn't send the phone back because I had not returned it within 90 days of receiving it. Under these unique circumstances, I felt that there should be an exception. But no one would budge—it was the company's *policy*.

I was transferred to three other departments. I spent over an hour on the phone until I finally found someone who appeared to understand the situation, told me he would investigate, and get back to me. He never did.

The next month when my bill came, another charge was on my bill. I called again and repeated my story. The CSR told me that there was nothing he could do and that I could not send the phone back. I clarified what he was telling me: "You mean to tell me that there is nothing, absolutely nothing, you can do, and that I am stuck paying for a phone I cannot use that I tried to return, but couldn't?" "That's right," he said. I asked to speak to his supervisor, but he refused, telling me that no one would help me. I couldn't believe my ears. He was doing absolutely everything someone in customer service *shouldn't* do. He interrupted me, didn't listen, refused to take any responsibility—or ownership—for my problem, acknowledge my frustration, or offer any type of solution.

After I hung up the phone, I immediately called back and talked with a supervisor. Although it took some time, I did eventually get permission to return the phone and had the charges removed from my bill. It was an experience I will never forget.

Successful Service Stories

I was at a training convention in San Francisco, and a few conventioneers and I were in a taxi on our way to dinner. The hotel I was staying at was across from a wonderful shopping area and earlier, on my way back from the convention, I had stopped to shop. I ended up spending most of my time at Nordstrom. You may or may not be aware of the wonderful reputation Nordstrom has acquired over the years, but this retailer is legendary for providing great service.

I talked about my shopping experience as we rode in the taxi and how pleasant it had been. Everyone had similar Nordstrom stories to share. For 20 minutes we talked and raved about Nordstrom and how they "get it" when it comes to service. Nordstrom couldn't have paid for better advertising.

I've heard Nordstrom stories for years, but until they entered the Minneapolis market several years ago, I hadn't experienced the store firsthand. I can't even tell you what it is, but when I walk into a Nordstrom store in any market, my experience is consistently pleasant. The salespeople have a *desire* to help. They have the ability to make decisions based on their own judgment if it helps to take care of their customers. Nordstrom is a great place to shop and I'm sure it is a great place to work as well!

I've had many incredible service experiences, and rather than take them for granted when things have been superb, I have taken the time to let the business know.

The Basics of Good Service

Many people feel that customers have become difficult and demanding and are the reason good service is declining. There are some people who truly are impossible to please. However, if you find that the majority of the people you come into contact with respond to you negatively, consider taking a look at yourself and the way you come across to others. Some people bring out the best in others. Others, because of their attitudes, bring out the worst.

Service comes down to one basic premise: *satisfying your customer.* Rather than focusing solely on your policies and what you want, focus on *your customers' wants and needs.* Granted, you can't please everyone, but you can increase your average.

More often than not, if you ask an unhappy customer what it is he or she wants, you will find that most simply want what is fair. Because so many people choose to avoid confrontation, many service people fail to respond to complaints and leave unhappy customers wondering why no one cares.

If you find that the majority of the people you come into contact with respond to you negatively, consider taking a look at yourself and the way you come across to others.

Last year my husband and I took a much-needed vacation to Palm Desert, California, our favorite travel destination. Prior to checking out of one of the city's finest hotels, I spoke by phone to the manager about an error on the bill. He offered to adjust our bill, but when we went to check out, the adjustment hadn't been made.

The trouble started when I began to question the front desk clerk about the bill. She was totally unprepared to deal with any type of problem. She became so uncomfortable that I felt as though she couldn't wait to get rid of us. She went in the back office for help and left us standing there feeling like criminals. Not only did she refuse to give us the adjustment that we had been promised, she never said thank you, good-bye, or come again.

I was so upset that I called the manager I had talked with that morning from the car as we left the hotel. He apologized and told me he would find out what happened and get back to me, but he never did. Two weeks later I called and talked to the assistant manager of the hotel who seemed genuinely concerned about what I had been through. He handled the call beautifully and informed me that I would receive the adjustment on my credit card and a letter of apology from him. Two weeks went by with no adjustment and no letter.

Out of desperation (and principle), I wrote a letter to the home office. This billing error, which began as a minor price adjustment, had now escalated to an enormous customer service problem. I was treated rudely, several people made promises but never followed through, and I was investing far too much time trying to get back what was rightfully mine.

Finally, after contacting the home office, the credit was issued and I received a letter of apology, including a free weekend stay at the hotel in the future.

Sounds great, doesn't it? Well, it wasn't. When we decided to return the following year, I called to book a weekend but was unable to, because there were limited days that I was allowed to use the certificate. As a result, what they offered to try to make things better ended up making things worse. In fact, all of the negative memories of my calls and frustrations were returning, and trying to explain became impossible. It was no longer worth the effort, and I vowed never to return to that hotel again. And while I am not mentioning the name of the hotel in this book, believe me, I have mentioned it to many others.

Unhappy customers shouldn't be viewed as a threat. Anytime someone is gracious enough to tell you what is wrong, use it as an opportunity to learn and make the services you provide even better.

What Do Customers Want and Expect?

So, what do customers want? First of all, customers want to be viewed as unique individuals. They want to be viewed as something more than just another person in line, another voice on the phone, or another order on a piece of paper or computer monitor. Customers are no different than you or I. Most customers' needs are fairly basic. They want to be acknowledged by a friendly, kind, and caring professional. They want to feel important and appreciated.

Customers Need to:
- Feel important.
- Feel valued.
- Feel good about spending money with you.
- Feel as though they are treated fairly.
- Be acknowledged.
- Be greeted with a hello, good morning, or good afternoon.
- Be treated in a friendly, professional manner.
- Be able to ask questions.
- Have questions answered.
- Have phone calls returned.
- Have problems resolved quickly.
- Deal with someone who can make decisions.
- Have expectations met or exceeded.

Customers want to be viewed as unique individuals. They want to be viewed as something more than just another person in line, another voice on the phone, or another order on a piece of paper or computer monitor.

Customers Detest:
- Being told "no."
- Waiting.
- Employees with bad attitudes.
- Apathetic service providers.
- Incompetent workers.
- Unfulfilled promises.
- Service people talking on the phone or visiting with friends.
- Seeing people eat on the job.
- Hearing someone tell them "I don't know."
- Lack of attention.
- Slow service.
- Being unappreciated.
- Being challenged.

Free to Serve

I had a lunch date with my friend Carol at an upscale restaurant. We planned to meet at 11:30 AM in order to avoid the lunch rush. Carol arrived a few minutes before me. She asked to be seated, but the hostess told her that it was against the restaurant's policy to seat partial parties. The restaurant wasn't at all busy, but the lobby was crowded with people waiting for the other members of their party to arrive. There was nowhere to sit, and my friend had a bad back that was made worse by standing.

Carol really wanted to sit down and order a drink, but the hostess refused to seat her. She commented that she thought the hostess was being rude but received no reply. The hostess then turned her back on my friend and began whispering about the situation to a coworker.

When I arrived, Carol was visibly upset. It's interesting how a slight altercation in a service establishment can have such a strong effect on both the server and the customer. Customers have a vested interest in the treatment they receive because they are paying a price for service. Servers *should* have a vested interest because without satisfied customers eventually their jobs will cease to exist.

Customers need to know that you understand their problem.

Too often service providers are more concerned about their policies than pleasing their customers. I am not suggesting that policies are meant to be broken or that you should allow customers to take advantage of you, but there is a big difference between being flexible and being rigid. The problem in this situation was more about the indifference of the hostess than about the restaurant's seating policy.

So what options did the hostess have? First, she could have empathized with my friend and validated her feelings. For example, imagine if she had started out by saying, "I am so sorry that I am unable to seat you, and I do understand how frustrating it is to stand." Rather than ignore her and whisper about her to coworkers, she would be showing compassion. Customers need to know that you *understand* their problem. Perhaps the hostess was prohibited from seating any incomplete parties under any circumstance. You might think she is stuck, but at this point, her creativity, flexibility, and *willingness to serve* come into play. She could say, "If you are thirsty and want to sit down, you are welcome to have a seat at the bar" or "I would be happy to order you a drink and bring it to you here." Now, the hostess has addressed all of the customer's concerns and, although not giving in, has made an offer to try to meet her needs.

If the hostess had any leeway in this situation, the best thing to do would have been to give my friend (the customer) what she wanted. She could have said, "I am so sorry we have no seats for you in the waiting area. I understand how painful it must be since you have a bad back, so I will go ahead and seat you." Now the customer feels privileged to be able to be seated, knowing that it is not the norm but because she, as a customer, is so valued. That is the way to please customers and generate positive comments.

Unfortunately, many service providers feel powerless and often merely recite the rules they have been told to memorize. If you provide service, you *must be free to serve*. Find out what decisions are within your power. I find it hard to believe that the hostess would have been reprimanded for seating my friend. Certainly, once she explained the circumstances, even her manager would have praised her for doing the right thing and encouraging a return visit by the customer.

If you are restricted from bending the rules in order to serve, you can still do more than say no to a customer: you can empathize and understand. Telling a customer that you understand is an instant way to break down barriers. If you do not have the power to give a customer what he or she needs, then find someone who can.

Anything is better than telling a customer no. You could say, "I really wish I could" or "I am so sorry I am unable to help you." Then try to offer something in return. The hostess could have said, "I really appreciate your understanding. Since I can't seat you right now, please let me buy you a drink [or a dessert] once you are seated as a small token of my appreciation for your understanding."

Always try to do something above and beyond the expected. This will come as an unexpected surprise and typically dis-

If you do not have the power to give a customer what he or she needs, then find someone who can.

arm an angry customer. If you are the one to offer a solution, you become the hero. And, you may find that the customer won't even accept the offer but will appreciate it because it shows your concern.

Don't Know

In addition to being told no, customers dislike hearing "I don't know." If you think about it, telling someone you don't know is the equivalent of telling someone you don't care. If you don't know an answer to a question, you can most certainly find out the answer. You have many resources available to you; use them.

Whether you're helping internal or external customers, *service* is the key.

Test Your Customer Service Skills

Questions and Answers

True or False?

1.

Most customers won't tell you when they are dissatisfied.

True. Only 4 percent of dissatisfied customers will take the time to tell you they are unhappy. It is much easier to walk away and do business somewhere else than it is to take the time to complain. Customers will feel no obligation to you unless you have attempted to establish a relationship with them. This means you need to do whatever you can to develop good relationships with your customers and to be attuned to your customers' reactions and feelings.

2.

One of the best ways to deal with an upset customer is by listening.

True. When a customer comes to you upset, just listen. If a customer feels wronged, he or she needs to tell you why. Don't jump in with your defense or tell your customer why he or she is wrong. By listening you are showing that you care, and by your reaction you show that you empathize with your customer. You will have a chance to talk, but don't begin until your customer has spoken.

3.

One word a customer never wants to hear is *no*.

True. When you tell a customer *no*, you are basically saying, "I will not do anything for you." *No* is final, and a customer service problem should never end before you have tried to resolve it. As a service provider, it is up to you to find a way to help and find some alternative solution if you cannot do what the customer wants. Be creative, flexible, and willing to serve.

4.

An angry customer is likely to tell three to five other people about his or her experience.

False. An angry customer is likely to tell as many as 20 other people about his or her experience. This is why you don't want to leave a customer enraged. When customers feel that you didn't listen to or meet their needs, they have a need to get the frustration off their chest and will do so by telling other people who will listen. Although you can't please everyone every time, you can do your best to resolve problems you are facing.

5.

Rules should never be broken.

False. Think of rules and policies as guidelines. While there may be some rules that are carved in stone, when it comes to making a customer happy, you should be given some flexibility. Know what options you have that give you the flexibility you need to serve before you encounter a problem.

6.

Coworkers can be considered customers, too.

True. Get into the habit of serving, whether with an external or internal customer. Doing favors for others, helping out, and being friendly are ways to establish good habits and get along well with others.

7.

Always thank a customer at the end of a transaction or conversation.

True. Saying thank you is a common courtesy and the best way to show appreciation to a customer. I make it a habit of thanking someone for helping me when I am the customer and am appalled at how many times I get no thanks in return. Saying thank you is easy to do, yet so often forgotten. Remember to end all of your transactions with a sincere thank you.

Chapter Summary

Remember, in Order to Provide Service You Need to

Satisfy
Empathize
Respond
Validate
Interact
Care
Excel

✓ **Satisfy** your customers and you will have people coming back for more. Dissatisfy your customers, and you will surely lose them. Even when you can't give someone what he or she wants, you can offer another solution. Let your customers know that their problems are no problem for you to handle. Use your creativity as you look for solutions to problems.

✓ **Empathize** with your customers. When someone is upset, empathy on your part is often all it takes to calm the person down. Listen to your customers without interrupting. Empathize with them by making statements such as "I can understand your frustration" or "I can see why this has upset you." Challenging or disagreeing with a customer creates an adversarial relationship between you and the customer. You will have much more success in resolving problems if you stay on the same side as your customer, which is what empathizing will help you do.

✓ **Respond** to your customers. Be responsive in your dialogue by asking customers questions and listening to their responses. If you don't have the answer to a question, never say, "I don't know"; say, "I don't have the answer, but let me find out for you," and do it. If you say you will get back to someone in an hour, get back to that person as you promised, even if you don't have the answer. Don't wait for a customer to complain or ask for something. If you know there is something that needs to be done, do it. Take the initiative. Keep your promises to your customers.

✓ **Validate** your customers. If customers are confused about something, don't make them feel inept. Validate them by saying, "These instructions can be confusing. Let me explain what we mean." If customers are upset, saying, "I agree with you" or "You have every right to be upset" will help the customers see that you are on their side.

✓ **Interact** with your customers. Whether on the phone or in person, greet your customers like friends. Always begin by saying hello and trying to find out what your customers need. If you sense something is wrong, make an effort to find out what it is. Get to know your customers by taking an interest in them and interacting with them. If you can, get to know the names of your repeat customers and greet them personally each time they visit or call your business.

✓ **Care** about your customers. Let your customers know you care by your sincere desire to please. Be sensitive to people who are in a hurry or who have had a bad experience. Make it your responsibility to connect with your customers and care enough to make sure they have their needs met.

✓ **Excel** in everything you do. Don't settle for status quo. Make it your goal to exceed customer expectations. When a customer gets more than he or she expected, you get more than a satisfied customer, you get a loyal customer.

Chapter 9

Sticky
Situations

True or False?

1.

As long as you do everything right, you won't encounter any problems at work.

2.

If you have a problem with someone, the best thing to do is to talk with that person.

3.

If you are offered another job and your new employer wants you to start immediately, it is fine to quit your job without notice.

4.

It is a good idea to have an exit interview when leaving a company.

5.

If you are having problems with a coworker, speak to his or her supervisor.

6.

Expect to have a job performance review and get raises every three to six months.

Test yourself as you read through this chapter. The answers appear on pages 230-231.

Working with Difficult People

Throughout this book I have reinforced the importance of remaining positive, friendly to others, and open to the changes that take place in your worklife. Even when you do everything in your power to be the right type of person, you are likely to encounter some challenges over the years.

You will likely develop friendships with many of your coworkers. In fact, you may discover that the people at work become like a second family. You will see the members of this "family" day in and day out, much more than you see anyone else, be it a real family member or friend. However, there can be disagreements and differences in the closest of relationships. So don't be surprised if and when something goes wrong or problems surface.

One theme I hear over and over again in the letters I receive for my advice column is how difficult some people can be to work with. Difficult people often change the dynamics of an entire office, and their behavior profoundly impacts their coworkers. It is interesting how one person often has the power to destroy the morale of an entire department. As a result, it is easier for some people to leave a bad situation than to stay and continue to work with a difficult person.

If you are afraid to stand up to someone or speak your mind, in essence, you are giving the other person control.

You can be assured that you will end up working with some people you like less than others, and some who are downright nasty. However, don't let the less pleasant people or the issues that arise get the best of you. Difficult people thrive on being difficult. Some people know no other way to get attention, others manipulate people in order to maintain control, and some people simply never learned the art of getting along with others.

What to Do When You Are Having Problems

Realizing that it is not a matter of *if* you will face problems but *when*, you may as well prepare yourself for some of the challenges that lie ahead. Although uncomfortable for many, speaking up about a problem is your best defense. If you are afraid to stand up to someone or speak your mind, in essence, you are giving the other person control. Never give away your power or let someone else determine what you do or how you feel.

Assume for a moment that Jim, a coworker you have been working with on a project, has been taking credit for everything, including your achievements. The last straw came when you were in a meeting and Jim announced *his* new idea and, as a result, received a promotion for his initiative and creativity. You are fuming because you were the one who came up with the idea. What would you do?

You may be tempted to talk about this situation with others, but the person you need to talk with is the one who did this to you. If you can react quickly enough, you are best off responding at the very moment something happens. You could say, "Thanks for remembering to bring that up, Jim. I came up with this idea last week when I realized we were over budget and knew it could save us a lot of time and money on the project."

If you can't bring yourself to address this issue in front of others or when it happens, make it a point to tell Jim that you are aware he is taking credit for your ideas and that you will not tolerate it. Give him the benefit of the doubt: "Jim, I realize we've been moving at a fast pace, but I hope you didn't forget that I was the one who thought of the idea you brought up at the meeting today. I think it is important that all of us are recognized for our contributions."

While you don't want to appear overly sensitive or as though you lack the ability to work as part of a team, you do need to make sure that your contributions are acknowledged. Some people are too overt in their attempts to gain recognition, while others are much too insecure and never give themselves the credit they deserve.

The Art of Self-Promotion

Self-promotion can be defined in many ways. There are people who manage to toot their own horn and delight in talking about their accomplishments. However, many people feel uncomfortable talking or boasting about what they have done.

Many people tend to minimize their strengths and accomplishments. Think about the conversations you have with others. Do you build yourself up or dwell on your shortcomings? Do you find opportunities to make things happen or wait until opportunities come to you? Are you willing to take on challenges and help out even when you may not benefit directly?

Self-promotion is more than tooting your own horn. In fact, someone who is effective at promoting him- or herself often does it in a way that isn't obvious to others and doesn't seem self-serving.

Self-promoters are often leaders who have an ability to energize others and make other people look and feel good. Many people refrain from complimenting others because they fear that it will detract from their own accomplishments. However, when you make someone else look good, you look good as well, and it reflects positively on you. Self-promoters are confident people who present themselves in the best possible manner at all times. They are also people who are willing to share credit and compliment the achievements of others.

For example, if you were to approach Jim, it would be beneficial to acknowledge something he has done so that it doesn't appear as though you are taking away the spotlight. In addition to reminding him that the idea he is claiming ownership for originally came from you, you might add, "By the way, I don't think I would have come up with that idea if it hadn't been for your suggestion that we look at other options for suppliers. That was a great idea."

Self-promotion is a way of thinking and being. Remember, no one is looking out for you to ensure you look good or that your accomplishments are acknowledged. There is no need to brag or talk about yourself all the time, but do know your strengths and capitalize on them. And don't let other people overshadow you.

When you make someone else look good, you look good as well, and it reflects positively on you.

Own Your Power

If someone or something is bothering you, find a way to address it. For example, if a coworker has a habit of making remarks that you find degrading, say something. Rather than avoiding the person or becoming stressed every time he or she says something that you feel is offensive, deal with the situation directly by speaking up. Never allow anyone to have power over you. Own your power.

It is difficult to earn the respect of others if you don't respect yourself.

When you feel the need to address what could be a sensitive subject with someone, such as complaining about something someone has done, don't blame anyone. Instead, take ownership. For example, rather than saying, "You are so rude when you make comments like that," try saying, "I have to tell you that I really feel I am being put down when I hear comments like that." Speaking in terms of *I* rather than *you* is important and sounds like less of an accusation.

Even when the problem you are having is with a superior, it is important to address the situation directly. My daughter Stephanie worked as a nanny for a woman who was very demanding and, at times, condescending toward her. As much as I encouraged her to speak up and establish what she was and wasn't willing to do, Stephanie remained skeptical and afraid.

When I tried to help her identify the basis of her fears, she told me that her biggest fear was making this woman angry. "I don't want her to be mad at me," she told me. I tried to help her see that it didn't really matter if the woman got mad, because she (my daughter) was mad, too. Although Stephanie felt she was taking being taken advantage of, it was easier for her to deal with her own anger than to take on this woman's anger.

Sometimes the energy it takes to deal with a toxic situation or difficult coworker isn't worth it. It *is* easier to deal with your own anger than it is to take on the anger of someone else. However, you will never get what you want if you always take the easy way out. It is easy to say nothing, but not the best way.

It is difficult to earn the respect of others if you don't respect yourself. By setting boundaries and addressing issues that are important to you, you make a statement about how you feel about yourself. This can be done quietly and politely, and there is no need to put down others in the process. People will treat you the way you expect to be treated.

Always be sensitive to the timing of your discussion when you decide to approach someone about a problem. Don't barge into someone's office and jump into a discussion when the mood strikes. Tell the person ahead of time that you need to talk and ask when it would be a good time to do so. Be sensitive to your coworkers and do your best to find a quiet place to talk where you won't be interrupted.

If you have no luck and nothing changes once you've addressed the issue with the person you are having the problem with, you may need to go to your supervisor. It is important for you to honor the hierarchy within your organization and to follow the appropriate chain of command. You risk alienating too many people if you don't.

One of the most important things to remember is that people will take advantage of you as long as you allow them to. Establish boundaries, stand up for what you believe and, if something is a problem for you, address it. Address issues while they are small, before they escalate into bigger problems. Follow these rules of productive discussion:

- Be direct, but not defensive.
- Be assertive, but not accusatory.
- Be specific, but not nitpicky.

Raises, Promotions, and Reviews

I will never forget Bernie, one of my first bosses. Bernie was a nice person, but he never felt comfortable managing people. He just wanted to be everyone's friend.

Bernie rarely commented on my job performance, but I sensed he was happy with my effort.

One Friday afternoon before we left for the day, Bernie asked me to help him carry some products to the storage room. We were putting away samples, talking and laughing. He said, "You know, Sue, I've never met your parents, but they sure did a good job raising you. You really have a good work ethic."

I felt funny inside. It was a little embarrassing to receive a compliment—especially from Bernie. I knew it was hard for him to put into words what he was thinking, and I knew he was doing his best to tell me that he appreciated the work I did. I thanked Bernie for his compliment and even passed on his kind words to my parents.

Everyone wants to be appreciated, and if we fail to get positive feedback from our bosses, we may become insecure

Address issues while they are small, before they escalate into bigger problems.

about the work we do. But many people are uncomfortable giving out compliments or simply don't know how. It is much easier for some people to tell you what you're not doing or what you're doing wrong than it is to tell you what you are doing right. In fact, some bosses believe that giving a compliment or positive feedback is unnecessary because it is expected that a person will do their job well.

If you find yourself working for someone who is stingy with praise and positive feedback, you may have to find ways to bring praise on yourself. While you don't want to appear needy, there is nothing wrong with checking in with your boss from time to time to inquire how you are doing.

When you are having a review it is important to stay calm and to be objective.

Typically, management will conduct periodic reviews of your development on the job. The length of time between reviews varies from company to company. Participate in your review as much as you can by planning ahead. Compile a list of issues you would like to discuss in detail, such as new assignments, a salary increase, a more flexible work schedule, or advancement opportunities. Don't assume your boss knows everything you do or have done. You may need to remind him or her of the projects you have worked on or the new responsibilities you have mastered since your last review. It also might be useful to create a list of your recent workplace accomplishments for reference during the review.

Reviews are important, and good reviews often lead to a pay raise. If your supervisor doesn't give you either, you may need to request one or the other. I realize that asking for a raise or a review can be difficult, but if you don't ask, you may not receive. No one will look out for you if you don't look out for yourself. Be your own advocate.

When you are having a review it is important to stay calm and to be objective. Determine any action you need to take to improve. Be involved in the discussion as much as possible. Accept any criticism as constructive and avoid the temptation to protect yourself by being too defensive.

Calling in Sick

I've always wondered what would happen if I were sick on a day I was expected to lead a workshop. For years I was able to tell people that I had never canceled an engagement. I'd given talks and spent days training with the flu, bad colds, and headaches, but always figured that the show must go on and somehow I'd pull through.

Then it happened. I woke up one morning and the room was spinning. I tried to get ready, but became so weak that I had to sit down every few minutes. I was dizzy and nauseous. The thought of driving my car to the workshop was too much to think about. I felt even sicker when I thought about standing and presenting all day.

I called the coordinator of the program and told her that I wouldn't be able to make it. People arrived for the seminar and were sent away. I felt awful thinking about the inconvenience I caused, but there was nothing I could do. I really was ill, and I was heartsick about canceling. I took solace in the fact that missing the seminar was an anomaly. I knew that no one questioned my motives or integrity.

Imagine, however, if I cancelled programs every time I had a headache or a sniffle or what if I cancelled just as many times as I knew it was allowed or until I would likely be reprimanded. That would be wrong. Most companies allow a certain number of sick days, and most managers understand the occasional illness and absence.

If you are frequently sick, even if it is by no fault of your own, you risk being viewed as weak, vulnerable, or undependable. Don't abuse your sick days or claim to be sick when you are not. If you ever do have a prolonged illness or become seriously ill, you will likely find people to be understanding and supportive as long as you haven't created a pattern that has led to mistrust.

Don't abuse your sick days or claim to be sick when you are not.

Obviously, good attendance is important, but through no fault of your own, you will undoubtedly come down with a cold or the flu at some point in your worklife. When you are really sick do yourself and everyone else a favor by staying home until you are well. If you go to work sick, and are sneezing and coughing, you spread germs to your coworkers. They will not appreciate it if you end up sick because you did not stay home.

When the Time Has Come for You to Leave Your Job

It is likely you will change jobs several times throughout your career. Leaving a job on good terms benefits you and your employer. However, it isn't always easy to make that happen.

Companies make changes all the time: buyouts, mergers, acquisitions, restructuring, and so on. You could be laid off or find yourself disillusioned at some point and ready to leave your job. In addition, due to performance or other issues, you may find yourself fired from your job. Under what circumstances is an employer allowed to fire an employee? According to Marshall Tanick, a lawyer and contributing editor on employment and labor law for *Bench & Bar,* the official magazine of the Minnesota State Bar Association, your employer's ability to fire you depends upon your employment status. People who have employment contracts, are members of labor unions, or work for the government generally cannot be fired unless there is "cause," which means serious misconduct. Most employees don't fit in these categories and are known as "at will" employees. Ordinarily, they can be fired for any reason at the discretion of management, provided that the discharge does not violate a specific law.

If you feel that your discharge is discriminatory or in violation of some other statute and you make a complaint with the appropriate agency, the employer must be able to show there were legitimate reasons for the discharge, such as poor work performance, failure to abide by company rules, economic or financial reasons, or any other business-related justification.

No one enjoys being fired or laid off. But there is a good chance that you will find another job that will be even better than the one you lost. Change can be a good thing. When you are hit with unexpected changes, look for the good in what is happening and ways in which you can benefit from it.

If you decide to leave a job, it is customary to give an employer a minimum of a two-week notice. This gives you a chance to tie up any loose ends and gives your employer a chance to fill your position and gather any and all necessary information (about the status of ongoing work projects or other work-related issues) from you.

It is fine to notify your employer of your intended departure in writing, but if possible, try to arrange a face-to-face conversation as well. While it is not necessary for you to go into too much detail about why you are leaving, it is always best to give a reason. Common reasons for leaving can be that you are ready for a new challenge, you were offered an exciting new opportunity, and your need to earn more money.

Speak Up When You Leave a Job

I visited my daughter Stephanie at her job recently and overheard her coworker saying she had just given her notice. When I asked her why, she told me it was because of her boss, who she felt was treating her unfairly. When I asked if she told her boss the reason for her departure, she said no. She used the excuse that it was too hard to keep up with her schoolwork and her job.

Apparently, she was too scared of this person and didn't see the purpose in giving a reason, assuming no one would care. She said a number of people had recently quit because of the way this boss treated people.

I encouraged my daughter's coworker to be honest about her reasons for leaving. How would her boss know there was a problem unless she spoke up? Who was she protecting anyway? While she didn't have to complain or be totally negative, a brief explanation would have been acceptable. If she didn't feel comfortable telling her boss, she could tell her boss's boss.

When You Are Let Go

If and when you are ever let go, it may be very uncomfortable for you as you work your remaining days on the job. Even though you are on your way out, keep in mind that you may work again with some of your coworkers or even your boss. You never know what opportunities will occur in the future.

I was called in by a company to present a series of seminars to 1,000 employees whose positions were likely to be eliminated. The reason I was called in was because the morale was so low that it was unbearable for those who were still working as well as those who were able to stay. The person who hired me knew that some of these people would be staying and that others would leave and end up in positions of authority elsewhere. What many of the employees failed to realize was that their performance on their way out could impact their future career opportunities. The people who were physically present but emotionally absent were not leaving with a very good impression.

I realize it is easier said than done to be positive and upbeat when you fear you are losing your job or have lost it, but what choice do you really have? As long as you are employed, work to your potential.

How Will You Know When It's Time to Go?

There are many reasons people choose to leave a job. Some people never seem to stay at any job for long, while others never seem to make any changes. There is no right amount of time for you to work at one particular job. While you don't want to become known as a job hopper or unstable, it is expected that you will have several jobs over the span of your career.

Too many people remain at their jobs simply because the work is easy and unchallenging or because they receive great pay and benefits. I'm frequently asked what to do when the passion and enthusiasm for a job is gone but the pay and security make it difficult to leave.

Money is important, but there are many ways to make money. So why not find a job that makes you happy, too?

What you should do will depend upon your situation at the time. If you dread going to work and find yourself not working to your capacity but sticking around for a paycheck, reconsider. Money is important, but there are many ways to make money. So why not find a job that makes you happy, too?

Any time you find yourself focusing more on what's wrong with your job than doing your job or you find yourself thinking negative thoughts most of the time, you ought to take a good look at what you are doing and why. Never allow a job to consume you or drain you, and always remain in control of yourself and the direction of your future.

You might consider looking for work elsewhere when:

✗ You dread going to work each day.

✗ You think and talk negatively about your job and company.

✗ You are bored and unchallenged.

✗ You have gone as far as you can go within your company.

✗ You have been denied your request for a promotion more than three times.

✗ You cannot remember the last time you received a raise.

✗ You have complained about things and have not seen any resolution.

✗ You resent your boss and others in management.

✗ You fantasize about working someplace else.

✗ You are just "getting by" and not working to your potential.

✗ You don't care any longer about the quality of your work.

✗ You don't receive any positive remarks about your work.

✗ You are getting complaints about your work or attitude.

✗ You've outgrown your position.

Leaving a Job in a Professional Manner

It is important to start a job on a positive note and equally important to end your job positively. Your image and the impression you create will follow you wherever you go. Whether you are happy or unhappy to leave your job, whatever you do, don't destroy your reputation or leave a negative last impression.

Even when you are down to your last few days of work, keep in mind that you are still working and still being paid. You may be "out of there" emotionally, but physically you are still present and professional behavior is expected at all times.

Some people develop a "who cares" attitude, assuming that they will never see any of their coworkers again, but don't be so sure. The world of work is much smaller than it seems, and you are likely to run into people over time. This is why you don't want to burn any bridges or hurt any relationships. Your behavior may come back to haunt you.

In order to leave a job in a professional manner, do the following:

- Give a minimum of a two-week notice.

- Leave your work area clean and tidy.

- Leave user-friendly information and instructions related to your job.

- Offer to help train your replacement.

- Offer your phone number or e-mail address so that you can be available for questions in the future.

- Act professionally the entire time of your employment, including the last day.

- Leave on a positive note.

- Thank everyone who has been helpful and supportive to you.

Exit Interview

Your company may request an exit interview, or you can request one. This gives you the opportunity to bring closure to your departure. If you are asked specific questions about your reasons for leaving, be candid in your responses but not slanderous.

Although I urged my daughter's coworker to tell her boss the real reason for her departure, I would never suggest she slander her boss. There are ways to get a point across without sounding bitter and accusatory. After all, if you've never complained before or gone directly to the person with your complaints, it may seem unjustified or unfair. Besides, if you are too negative or angry, not only will your departure be justified, you will be the one who will end up looking poorly.

What to Do if You Are Being Harassed

Some of the hottest topics in corporate training have to do with respect in the workplace, understanding and dealing with diversity, and the prevention of harassment and discrimination. Companies want their employees to understand the importance of respecting diversity and to behave in a respectful and legal manner.

You've likely heard of some of the lawsuits that have been filed claiming harassment or discrimination. No publicity is worse than negative publicity for a company, which is why it is so important for companies to take a stand of zero tolerance toward harassment and discrimination. Yet, even with the best training in place and a strong stand against inappropriate behavior, incidents can and do happen.

If someone consistently acts in a manner that makes you feel uncomfortable or treats you differently than others, the first thing to do is to approach the person. However, if you truly fear this person or the repercussions of saying something, then it would be wise to go to that person's supervisor or to the human resources department. If you still are not satisfied, you may consider going to the company's legal department.

If you have been involved in a number of incidents, you will want to document them. The more information you have that supports your claim, the better. Try to do everything you can within the company before going outside the company to file a complaint.

You should never have to tolerate discrimination and harassment in the workplace or in any other area of your life. Although they are not required to by law, most companies have sexual harassment policies. The existence of a policy can help satisfy the courts, which have ruled that appropriate and preventive action in dealing with sexual harassment issues is required. If you are concerned about sexual harassment, find out if your company has a policy and understand its terms.

If your problem is not being resolved, Marshall Tanick suggests you go to the Equal Employment Opportunity Commission (EEOC), the federal agency that oversees the federal discrimination and harassment laws. The statute of limitations for filing such claims varies depending upon the state in which the incident occurs, but a claim usually must be filed within 180 to 300 days of the alleged harassment. Most states, and even some large cities, have statutes and ordinances that address sexual harassment issues in the workplace. Rather than filing a claim with the EEOC, you can file charges with either state or local agencies. The federal and state agencies where the claim is filed generally will conduct an investigation, attempt to resolve the matter through mediation or other conciliatory efforts, and ultimately make a determination as to whether there is "probable cause" to support the allegation. The agency also may assist employees who have meritorious claims to pursue their claims through the court system.

If you are concerned about sexual harassment, find out if your company has a policy and understand its terms.

As an alternative to these steps, you can pursue a lawsuit through private legal counsel. A claim cannot be pursued under the federal Civil Rights Act unless a charge is first filed with the EEOC and the EEOC is given 180 days to investigate the matter. However, lawsuits can be filed after the expiration of the 180-day period or, in most cases, can be filed in state courts without going through the EEOC.

Sexual harassment claims can be resolved through negotiations without going to court. If internal negotiations do not resolve the issue, parties can select their own method for

Useful Web Sites

Equal Employment Opportunity Commission
http://www.eeoc.gov/

The Age Discrimination in Employment Act of 1967
http://www.eeoc.gov/laws/adea.html

Americans With Disabilities Act Home Page
http://www.usdoj.gov/crt/ada/adahom1.htm

dispute resolution, such as arbitration or mediation, where the parties mutually select one or more persons to resolve the dispute without going to court. This process is less expensive than going through governmental administrative agencies or to court.

Questions and Answers

True or False?

1.

As long as you do everything right, you won't encounter any problems at work.

False. Chances are that you will encounter a few problems at work during the course of your career no matter how good a job you do. There may be times that in spite of your efforts you create a problem and will need to take ownership of it. Other times, the problem will be a result of someone else's doing. But if the problem affects you, you still need to take some ownership and resolve the issue.

2.

If you have a problem with someone, the best thing to do is to talk with that person.

True. As difficult as it often is, you are much better off going to the source of your problem than holding it in or talking about it to others. Discussing the problem is the only way to get to the bottom of the issue and reach a resolution.

3.

If you are offered another job and your new employer wants you to start immediately, it is fine to quit your job without notice.

False. It is inconsiderate and totally self-serving to quit without giving at least two weeks notice. If your new company wants you, it will wait and respect the fact that you are honoring your current commitment.

4.

It is a good idea to have an exit interview when leaving a company.

True. Some companies routinely request an exit interview. It helps bring closure to the relationship. In addition, an exit interview provides you with the opportunity to have your final say about what worked and what didn't work on the job.

5.

If you are having problems with someone, speak to his or her supervisor.

True. However, this should be done only after you have talked directly with the person you are having trouble with. If you make a habit of running to your supervisor with every complaint or problem, you will appear incapable of dealing with your own problems or, worse yet, be perceived as a chronic complainer.

6.

Expect to have a job performance review and get raises every three to six months.

False. While some companies have standard reviews and policies for raises, some do not. Find out the policy in your company, and if you don't receive a performance review or raise after a year, consider requesting them.

Chapter Summary

Remember:

✓ Own your power.

✓ If you have a problem with someone, go directly to the source.

✓ Follow the appropriate chain of command when you have a problem with a coworker. First, discuss the issue with the coworker. If the person is unwilling to discuss the issue or unwilling to change his or her behavior, then take the issue to your supervisor.

✓ If you need feedback from your boss but aren't getting any, ask for some.

✓ Don't call in sick if you're not, and don't go to work if you are.

✓ Be open to change.

✓ View criticism constructively.

✓ If you plan on leaving your job, give your employer at least a two-week notice.

✓ When leaving a company, try to leave on a positive note.

Chapter 10

Office Errata

True or False?

1.

If you need a pen, it is fine to borrow one from a coworker's desk.

2.

It you are romantically involved with a coworker, keep it quiet.

3.

Attendance at the company party or picnic is optional.

4.

If alcohol is served at a business function, it is okay to drink as much as you want.

5.

It's not a good idea to bring a casual date to a company party.

6.

Smokers are allowed to take extra breaks if they need a cigarette.

7.

You represent your company at all times, even when you are away from the office.

8.

Some companies won't hire or promote someone until a company representative and the person have dined together.

Test yourself as you read through this chapter. The answers appear on pages 244-245.

Maintaining Decorum in the Office

There are unspoken expectations in every workplace, some of which we have covered already in this book. Every office has its own sense of protocol, and it is important for everyone who works in the office to understand all the rules, both explicit and implied.

For example, there is a limit on the amount and type of physical contact you should have with a coworker. The only sure way to avoid offending others is by treating them respectfully. No physical contact, outside of a handshake, is recommended in the workplace. The days of patting someone on the back or offering a hug as a means of comfort are long gone. This is not to say that you can't hug someone if the occasion and the mood creates an appropriate tone, but don't make a habit of it and don't assume it is acceptable.

The safest and only universally acceptable physical contact in the world of work is the handshake. Make sure you take the opportunity to communicate emotion and strength through yours.

If someone touches you, no matter how innocently, and it makes you feel uncomfortable, speak up. Just because someone else chooses to hug or kiss you does not mean you have to allow it or reciprocate.

The safest and only universally acceptable physical contact in the world of work is the handshake.

Respecting Personal Space in the Office

If you step onto an elevator and someone else is already on, it is natural to find a spot that is a comfortable distance away from the other person. We all have a comfort zone of about three to six feet. When someone invades our space we become uncomfortable. If someone encroaches on our comfort zone during a conversation, we have a tendency to back up.

At work, your office or cubicle is your personal space—the only personal space you have. You will make this space "yours" by the way you organize it along with the photos, art, and sayings you display. Unless your desk is a total mess, you can probably tell if someone has been at your desk or gone through your belongings. If this is done without your permission, you will probably be offended.

Some people work very closely (literally) to others and long for whatever privacy they can get. Be sensitive to the need we all have for privacy. Consider the following privacy rules and do your best to respect the personal space of others:

Don't:
- Enter a coworker's cubicle without permission.
- Borrow something from a coworker's desk without permission.
- Use a coworker's phone without permission.
- Look through papers on a coworker's desk.
- Remove anything from a coworker's work area without permission.
- Stand at the entrance of a coworker's cubicle while he or she is engaged in a conversation with another person or on the phone.

Office Gossip

Office gossip is inevitable. People love to hear the scoop about their coworkers. Most of the time, what is said isn't good and has little to do with anything relevant to the work at hand. Perhaps talking about others takes the focus off of ourselves or our own inadequacies and shortcomings. However, if you depend on gossip and use it in your conversations with others, you risk your reputation.

While gossip of a general nature (vacations, family, office events) can be enjoyable, "harmful gossip" can be repetitive, hurtful, and very unproductive over time. Harmful gossip is any information or rumor that demeans the character and reputation of an individual. It is usually disseminated behind the subject's back, which doesn't allow the person a chance to refute or correct the information.

You are bound to hear your fair share of gossip in the workplace. Just because you hear gossip does not mean you have to respond to it. Don't take anything you hear too seriously, but do pay attention to what you hear. Most gossip is worthless, but some gossip can contain powerful information. Don't appear too eager to hear or participate in harmful gossip.

Whenever possible, avoid talking negatively about other people or repeating harmful gossip to others.

Office Romances

People often wonder where to go to meet people with similar backgrounds and interests. One of the most likely places to meet someone who has some of the same interests as you is at work.

If you develop a serious relationship with a coworker, keep it quiet. Don't get others involved; it could be especially difficult if the romance doesn't last. If you are looking to meet someone, be prudent. Don't become a big flirt or flaunt yourself as available. If a relationship evolves, fine, but don't try too hard to make something happen. Your work is a place of business, not high school or the college dorm. Do not talk about who you have a crush on or your first date or ask someone to set you up during business hours.

While some companies have strict policies against employee fraternization, many do not. Know your organization's policy on office dating.

If you develop a relationship with someone you work with, be discreet. Whatever you do, don't let your relationship interfere with your work. Refrain from holding hands, kissing, sneaking around, and other obvious displays of affection. Do your best to keep the details of your relationship private. If your relationship doesn't work out, you won't want to have to explain why to everyone.

If it becomes common knowledge that you are dating a coworker, remember that both of you will be watched more closely by your bosses and coworkers. Your relationship may become the subject of harmful gossip. Avoid becoming the subject of harmful gossip by conducting yourself in a professional manner at all times.

> *If you develop a relationship with someone you work with, be discreet. Whatever you do, don't let your relationship interfere with your work.*

Representing Your Company Professionally at All Times

When you are asked what you do, and you reply that you work for a certain company, in that moment you are the company.

No matter where you are or how far from the office you may be, you are representing the company you work for.

Happy hour, lunches, dinners, trade shows, and conventions are just some of the many places where you may find yourself representing your employer. Although many of these activities do not take place at work, they are work related.

Always look and act your best when representing your company at any type of workplace function.

Let's Party!

Working full-time takes a lot of time, effort, and commitment. It is essential that you enjoy what you do and helpful if you feel at ease with your coworkers and customers. One way in which people build bonds is by socializing after hours.

Going out with your buddies after work is fine. So is meeting for lunch and taking breaks together. It is likely that the conversation will not always center on business, but remember it still is a business-related event. You don't need to be too cautious or be on guard, but do be aware that what you say could be misconstrued or repeated to others to cast you in a bad light.

Always look and act your best when representing your company at any type of workplace function.

There are still boundaries. Just because you are in a bar doesn't mean you can suddenly act flirtatiously or less respectfully to others. Nor is it appropriate to tell "off-color" jokes or gossip about others.

One event that seems to stand out as a highlight of the year is the company holiday party. Mix a festive time of year, a party after hours, and plenty of free food and alcohol and you create a potential disaster.

Many women choose to wear their most festive (and sometimes revealing) dresses to the holiday party, but beware, the holiday party is still a business event. Would you show your cleavage at work during business hours? If not, then why would you consider dressing in a revealing way at your company's holiday party?

Know Your Limit

Do not drink too much at work-related events, even if alcohol is served and other people are drinking and getting drunk. Know your alcohol limit. Even when it appears as though everyone else is drinking, if you lose control you risk losing your good reputation.

I have heard too many disastrous stories about what alcohol can do to people at business events. Some people have lost their jobs as a result of their inappropriate behavior, while others have lost even more: the respect of others and their good reputation. Consider these examples of horrific office party behavior:

- A woman began to tease her boss about his hair. She got so drunk that she told him people suspected he wore a hairpiece and, ultimately, pulled it off his head!
- Two coworkers disappeared for a few minutes only to be found in an intimate embrace in the women's restroom.
- Two coworkers get into a knock-down, drag-out fight on the dance floor at a holiday party.

An incident that tops all of these stories took place at a company party held at a plush resort. Dinner was served, people were dancing and drinking, and a woman stood up on a table and began to do a striptease—down to her underwear. She was fired the next day.

These are just a few of the many unbelievable stories I have heard. These incidents took place at business events where alcohol was served. I honestly believe that none of these situations would have taken place without the influence of alcohol.

Never feel pressure to drink. My recommendation is that you don't drink. There is no need to explain why, but if you are pressured to provide a reason, you can blame it on medication, a headache, or the fact that you are a designated driver for the night. If you do decide to drink, know your limit and keep your drinking to a minimum.

Do not drink too much at work-related events, even if alcohol is served and other people are drinking and getting drunk. Know your alcohol limit.

To Smoke or Not to Smoke?

Smoking has lost its glamour and appeal in recent years due to its many negative side effects, yet some people continue to smoke. Many buildings are smoke free and there are fewer and fewer public places for smokers to smoke.

Smoking is often viewed negatively, and you may be viewed less favorably if you smoke. I received a letter from a reader who felt that it was unfair that smokers took more breaks than nonsmokers. After publishing the letter in my column, I received an enormous amount of mail on the subject. Many of my readers felt that smokers did take more breaks than nonsmokers. Whether this perception is true or not, it is clear that many people resent the additional breaks smokers seem to receive.

During my seminars, I've noticed that the smokers tend to wander in a few minutes late after breaks. Try not to let your smoking interfere with your work or productivity. In addition, make sure you don't reek of smoke. Take your breaks as far away from nonsmokers as possible. If you are required to smoke outside, don't stand in the doorway or in front of the building. This forces everyone who enters the building to inhale your smoke.

Table manners are important and reveal a lot about a person.

Use breath mints frequently and air out your clothes after you've worn them. Even when you can't smell smoke, the scent stays with you.

Dining Etiquette

If you don't watch your table manners, someone else will. Some companies won't even consider hiring or promoting someone until a company representative and the person have dined together. Table manners are important and reveal a lot about a person. If you are unsure about your behavior and mannerisms at the table, it's time to brush up on your skills.

No one expects you to be an etiquette expert. Embarrassing things can happen when you are eating, talking, and trying to maintain a sense of control. Food may become lodged in your teeth, strings of cheese may hang from your mouth, utensils may drop on the floor, and something is bound to spill. Not one of these things will dismiss you as a candidate for a job or cost you your reputation. However, your reaction to these events is what people will notice and, as a result, judge you on.

You want to appear savvy and knowledgeable. Pay attention to other people and the way in which they handle themselves during a meal. If you eat in front of the television, slurp your soup, gobble down a meal within five minutes and think that the louder the belch, the bigger the compliment to the chef, it will be difficult for you to put on the charm when you need to. Learn by observing others and by practicing good habits every day.

Ideas to Chew On

Keep the following tips in mind as you attend business meals:

- Always arrive a few minutes early for a business lunch or dinner. There is no such thing as fashionably late in business.
- When deciding what to order, choose something easy to eat. Avoid triple-decker sandwiches, spaghetti, or any food that requires skill and focus.
- If you are unsure about what to order, ask the waiter for suggestions.
- If you are unsure about which plate to use, observe what others are doing. Remember your beverages will be on your right and your bread plate on your left.
- If you are unsure which utensil to use, observe what others are doing or work from the outside of your silverware setting in.
- Place your napkin on your lap immediately after being seated.
- If you need to leave the table during the meal, place your napkin on the chair.
- Keep your napkin on your lap until it is time to leave, then place it neatly on the table.
- Don't order the most expensive item on the menu.
- Don't order too lightly. Ordering a bowl of soup while everyone else eats full meals will draw attention to you and could make you appear nervous or uncomfortable.
- If you have special dietary needs, be discreet when discussing them and don't make them a big issue.
- If there is a problem with your food or your order, quietly inform your waiter.

- If you haven't been served but others at your table have, tell them to start eating.
- Wait to begin eating until at least half of the people at the table have been served or until you've been invited to do so by others who have not yet been served.
- Turn off your cell phone and pager during the entire meal.
- Do not pick your teeth or use a toothpick at the table.
- Learn the proper way to hold and use your utensils. Never shovel food in your mouth.
- Do not talk with your mouth full of food.
- Dab, rather than wipe, your face with the napkin provided.
- Do not put lipstick on at the table.
- Do not blow your nose at the table.
- Don't burp.
- Don't reach across the table if you need something; ask a neighbor to pass the item.
- Always pass the bread and butter; don't allow it to get stuck in front of you.
- If someone asks for the salt, pass the pepper, too.
- If you plan on treating, make arrangements in advance to avoid any argument over who pays the bill.
- Avoid commenting on others' food or the bill.

Socializing Dos and Don'ts

Whether it's a meeting, convention, holiday party, or the company picnic, it helps if you arrive prepared. Knowing the names of people who will be there and having something to talk about will help you interact with others and feel comfortable. Company parties typically include spouses or significant others, and you need to help make your guest feel comfortable, too.

The following guidelines will help you to become a socializing success.

Do:

- Introduce yourself to people you do not know well.
- Stand as much as possible to help you appear more approachable to others.

- Stay close to your date, especially if he or she has not met your coworkers before.
- Make proper introductions and provide some information for the basis of a conversation.
- Stick with light conversational topics.
- Always keep your right hand free (and dry) for a handshake when greeting others.
- Wear a name badge (if provided) on your right side.
- Move around the room rather than plopping yourself down in one spot for the evening. This will enable you to mingle and talk with different groups of people.
- Have something to eat before the event; you will tolerate alcohol better if you drink and won't feel the need to stuff your face.

Don't:

- Drink to get drunk.
- Wear suggestive or revealing clothing.
- Flirt, especially with someone else's date or spouse.
- Hover over the buffet table or stuff your face. While food is included, it isn't and shouldn't be the main attraction.
- Bring a casual date to an office party or event. You may find yourself preoccupied as you try to explain who's who or find that this person is an embarrassment and doesn't represent you well.
- Engage in gossip or talk badly about people.
- Complain, whine, or moan about your job, your coworkers, or the food or music at the event.
- Brown-nose or brag about your accomplishments.
- Monopolize the conversation or talk too much about yourself.

Questions and Answers

True or False?

1.

If you need a pen, it is fine to borrow one from a coworker's desk.

False. Do not borrow anything from anyone's desk without permission.

2.

If you are romantically involved with a coworker, keep it quiet.

True. You don't want attention to be diverted from your skills and on-the-job achievements to your love life. If you do become romantically involved with a coworker, be discreet and don't let your relationship interfere with your work.

3.

Attendance at the company party or picnic is optional.

False. No one will tell you attendance is mandatory, but you should attend unless you have a good reason not to. If you fail to attend and don't have a valid reason, management may conclude that you don't care or that you lack company spirit. Show your camaraderie and participate in company events.

4.

If alcohol is served at a business function, it is okay to drink as much as you want.

False. People who drink too much often lose control; people who lose control are of no value to a company. If you choose to drink, limit your alcohol intake. It is fine not to drink at all.

5.

It's not a good idea to bring a casual date to a company party.

True. If you aren't seriously involved with someone, you are probably better off attending the party alone. Unless you know the person well, you won't know what to expect from your date. The expected is much safer than the unexpected at a business event.

6.

Smokers are allowed to take extra breaks if they need a cigarette.

False. Smokers should not take any additional or longer breaks than anyone else.

7.

You represent your company at all times, even when you are away from the office.

True. Many events, such as lunches, dinners, meetings, and conventions, take place away from the workplace but are work related. It is important to keep this in mind and represent your company professionally and positively no matter where you are.

8.

Some companies won't hire or promote someone until a company representative and the person have dined together.

True. The way you handle yourself in conversation and at the table enables others to learn more about the real you. Brush up on your conversational skills and table manners so that you add to and not detract from your overall image.

Chapter Summary

Remember:

✓ Other than a handshake, touch is considered taboo in the workplace.

✓ Respect the personal space of others. Don't take anything from a coworker's desk or enter another employee's cubicle without permission.

✓ Pay attention to the gossip you hear, but don't be the one to spread the news.

✓ Be discreet if you become involved romantically with a coworker.

✓ Represent your company in the most professional manner at all times.

✓ Attend company functions.

✓ Limit your alcohol intake or avoid alcohol altogether at company functions.

✓ Don't let smoking interfere with your work.

✓ Brush up on your dining etiquette.

A f t e r w o r d

The seminar I was teaching began promptly at 8:30 AM. It was 9:15, and the seminar was well underway when a man and a woman entered the room. They moved through the rows of people, trying to find a place to sit. I did my best to continue with the program, but it was difficult to ignore the commotion they were causing. The woman wore a large brimmed hat and dressed in a combination of spandex and workout gear. She complained loudly about the fact that they couldn't find two seats together. She finally found a place in the back of the room and grunted as she plopped her things down, while the man moved to an open seat in the front of the room. He was breathing heavily, and once he sat down, he pulled out an asthma inhaler and began taking deep loud breaths. Heads were turning in both directions, but I was determined to continue for the sake of the other 50 people in the seminar.

The man was intrusive and didn't hesitate to interject his comments as I spoke or have side conversations with the people seated near him. On several occasions he blew his nose so loudly as I was talking that I felt compelled to repeat myself for the benefit of those who couldn't hear. I couldn't believe my eyes when the woman in the back pulled out a newspaper and began reading it, holding it high enough for everyone to see and turning the pages loudly enough to attract the attention of those who did not.

During breaks, the man monopolized my time. As we talked, the woman loudly repeated his name, encouraging him to join her outside for a smoke. He was oblivious to the fact that others were waiting to speak with me and did nothing to wrap up the conversation. It was evident that these people were irritating others in the class, but no one, including me, knew what to do

These two people were so consumed in their own worlds that they were oblivious to the world around them. From the moment they entered the room, I knew that they were "different." The fact that they were so late, their overall demeanor, the way they dressed, and their lack of awareness and sensitivity to their surroundings were strong indications about what these people were all about.

That same day, as I was making phone calls, I was connected to the voice mail of a woman I needed to speak with. I listened as she explained the dates she would be out of the office and realized that her voice mail message was over three weeks old. It was the end of the month, and she was reciting her schedule for the beginning of the month! Perhaps it was a small oversight, yet it was one that was noticed, therefore enabling me to draw negative conclusions about this woman.

These may be small, even petty stories to recount, but each incident stands out in my mind. Everything you do has implications and sends a message to others about who you are.

Failing to update your voice mail is no crime. I can think of worse things to be criticized for. But what message does it send to callers? "I forgot," "I'm too busy," and "I don't pay attention to the little things" are just some of the conclusions that may be drawn.

It is easy to keep your voice mail current. It is easy to arrive somewhere on time. It doesn't take any additional time to pay attention to one's surroundings, dress appropriately, and act courteously and sensitively to others. So why don't more people pay attention to the little things that make a difference?

Perhaps they don't care or simply are indifferent. Indifference has the potential to destroy your career and your relationships. Indifference can negatively impact an entire company.

Everything you do has implications and sends a message to others about who you are.

In this book, I've given many examples of what *not* to do and have tried to provide balance by describing many things you *should* do to ensure success in your career and in your life.

I encounter rude or indifferent people every day, and for a moment, I pause and wonder how they got to be that way. Every time I experience a negative situation, it reaffirms the need for the work I do. But in no way have I lost faith in people, because, much more often, I encounter people epitomizing goodness and all that's right in the world, people who *make a difference* with their actions every day: the person who greets me with a smile and the one who sincerely offers to help me; the people who come up to me after a seminar to say thank you or share a personal story with me; the people who are willing to connect with me through their eyes and facial expressions; the people who enthusiastically embrace everything they do. I could go on and on. They may not always know it, but these people make a difference in the world we live in.

When you embrace what you do, when you do what you love, and when you choose to have a positive impact on others, you are rewarded personally, professionally, and often monetarily.

I began my business many years ago with the idea of helping others to help themselves. I may have been naïve about the amount of work involved, but I was passionate and believed in what I was doing. I cannot tell you how many times I have come close to giving up, wanting to throw in the towel and find a *real* job, one where I would have a place to go every day, people to work with, and a guaranteed paycheck.

Instead, I continued down my own path, with all of the ups and downs of working alone, trying to create something out of nothing.

For years, the money I made had to go back into the development of my business, and I wasn't receiving the financial rewards I thought I deserved. I would look at the bottom line and feel like a failure. Yet, when I looked at the momentum I was gaining, the positive feedback from customers, and the things I was able to accomplish, I saw nothing but success. I began to question the meaning of success. Was success based on the bottom line or fulfilling a purpose?

Indifference has the potential to destroy your career and your relationships.

Many people are after success, yet everyone defines success differently. Some people define success by the amount of money they make, others seek impressive titles and gauge their success by their climb up the corporate ladder. Some people feel successful if they are able to do work that is meaningful or make a contribution through the work they do.

For me, success is a journey, one that has pushed me to do things I never anticipated and helped me grow into the person I have become. I've tried to live by the philosophy that if you do what you love, the money will follow. I have found my purpose and my calling through my work. Although I can go for months at a time without much validation and sometimes more than my share of criticism, there are defining moments in which I sit back, smile, and take a deep breath after being reassured I am traveling down the right road and helping people.

Taking a stand on issues, speaking professionally, and writing books invite feedback, which isn't always favorable but is expected. After all, it is the variety of opinions that makes what I do interesting. However, kind words of encouragement always seem to come at just the right time, usually when I doubt my efforts or wonder if what I do can possibly make a difference. The following letter came at such a time:

> Dear Susan Morem,
> I am a soldier stationed at Fort Polk, Louisiana. Self-help books interest me and that is why I checked out your book, *How to Gain the Professional Edge,* from the library. I am a blue-collar worker who always wanted to know how to transform myself into a suit and tie kind of person. Your book taught me so much about work etiquette and how to treat others. With the knowledge I've gained from this book, my life will be forever changed. Thanks.

I read that letter and was in awe. I never expected such a letter, which is why it touched me so. This man was thanking me, but it wasn't really about me. He was open to learning and changing, and willing to do something to help himself. I was simply a catalyst.

I don't know all of my readers, and I will never know what impact my words have. I realize that I can make a difference through what I do, and I know that no matter what career field that you work in, you can, too. No matter what you do, you have the ability to make a difference, every single day.

I have devoted hours upon hours to writing this book and have included everything I know to be true: information that is not just my opinion but that has been proven time and time again by those who have succeeded and failed before you. You don't need to learn the hard way. You can make your journey easier by paying attention to the proven practices of successful people.

As you enter the world of work, I hope that you find your place in it. Work is a place for you to shine, to grow, and to enjoy what you do. Never give up until you find that place. Define success for yourself and find a way to achieve your dreams. No dream is impossible.

One of the challenges of writing this book is ending it. Of course I am glad to be through with the work involved. I feel a sense of accomplishment, but writing this book has been such a part of me that it is hard to let go. I want so much to help you help yourself. I hope you have found what you are looking for in this book and that this information makes a difference in your life.

For me this is an ending; for you, a beginning. I wish you a bright beginning that brings you happiness and success in everything you do!

Index